THE NATURE OF THE ISLANDS

Plants and Animals of the Eastern Caribbean

Note: In this book we mention many herbal remedies. We find aloe very effective as a first aid for burns, though rather staining on clothes. Apart from this, these herbal remedies are for interest only and should not be taken as prescriptions.

Library of Congress Cataloging-in-Publication Data

Barlow, Virginia,
The nature of the islands : plants and animals of the Eastern Caribbean / Virginia Barlow

ISBN # 0-944428-13-4

Library of Congress Card Number: 92-075541

© Virginia Barlow, 1993

Edited by Chris Doyle

Chris Doyle Publishing and
Cruising Guide Publications
P.O. Box 1017, Dunedin, FL 34697-1017
Phone: (813) 733-5322, Fax: (813) 734-8179

THE NATURE OF THE ISLANDS

Plants and Animals of the Eastern Caribbean

by
Virginia Barlow

Color illustrations by
Katie Shears

Photographs by
John Douglas
Virginia Barlow
Chris Doyle
Underwater photographs by
Joan Bourque

Black and white drawings by
Joan Waltermire
Chris Doyle

Edited by
Chris Doyle

Acknowledgements

I have been helped by many people, both while learning about Caribbean natural history in the islands and while putting this book together in Vermont. Chris Doyle pushed me into this project before I realized what I was getting into, but he has more than redeemed himself by helping me enormously from start to finish.

Jacques Daudin and his family (Union Island), Desmond Nicholson (Antigua), Arlington James (Dominica), William Gooding (Bequia), Maria Grech, Clare Nunn, Robert Devaux and Wayne Burke (St. Lucia), and Earl Kirby (St. Vincent) are among the many islanders who generously shared their knowledge of plants and animals.

John Donnelly, of the University of Vermont, was just trying to teach me forest ecology, but instead he inspired me to keep studying, long after the course was over. Shirley Grainger, of the Dartmouth College Library, helpfully pointed me in the right direction. Joan Waltermire untangled a lot of my sentences and Jennifer Tulloss helped root out innumerable small mistakes. Paul Tobias sorted out my computer from time to time. Sally and Chuck Jorgensen, Witt Barlow, Warren Loomis and John Douglas supplied just what I needed, just when I needed it.

I am interested in hearing from readers who find errors in the book or who have suggestions for a future edition (HCR 82, Box 170, Corinth, Vermont 05039).

TABLE OF CONTENTS

If tropical nature is new to you, you may have some of the same feelings you would have at a large party, where all the other guests are total strangers. Everything you see is a bit bewildering. But with the animals and plants, as with the partygoers, making just a couple of friends can be very gratifying, and this accomplishment may inspire you to identify a few more unknowns. Even plants have something akin to personality: a mix of traits derived from their appearance, how they mate and reproduce, their history, the uses to which they have been put in the past, and their complex relationships with other species and with the sites that they grow on. Once you learn to recognize a plant you will remember it, even if you forget its name. In this book we aim to get you at least on nodding terms with some of the more common and interesting island plants and animals.

The Windwards and Leewards lie dotted along an arc from Puerto Rico to Venezuela. The idea that they once formed a land bridge is appealing, but both geological and biological evidence suggests that most have been separated from the mainland since their formation. The islands mark the meeting of two tectonic plates. Beneath them, the westward-moving American plate is being pushed under the Caribbean plate, which is moving east. The pressure and friction of the collision has caused the earth's crust to melt and spew upwards. It is this volcanic activity which has created the islands.

Geologically these islands (except Barbados) form two distinct volcanic groups: an inner arc of steep volcanic islands and an outer arc of eroded volcanos which have been capped with thick limestone deposits. The main difference between the volcanic and limestone islands is age.

The steep islands are geologically young, probably less than 50 million years. They lie on a submerged ridge whose summit is now 3000 to 5000 feet below sea

6

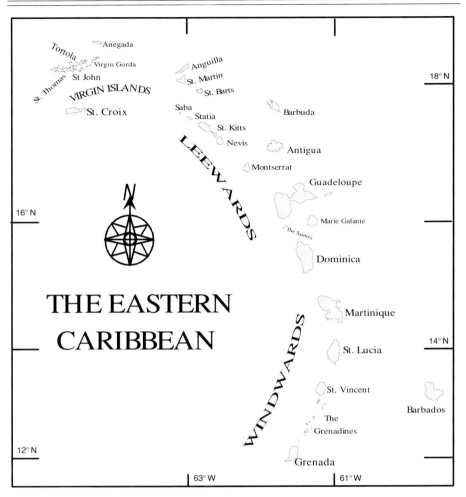

level. There are deep trenches between several of the major islands. These islands are all mountainous, often extremely so. As weather wears away at the mountains it rounds them off and the eroded sediments collect in the low lying areas around the coastal fringe. These deep soils are prized by farmers.

Volcanic eruptions have been mostly of the explosive type in which masses of rock and hot ash flows, called nuees ardents, were belched forth. Flows of liquid lava are rare, but many road cuts reveal rocks of all sizes embedded in a fine compacted ash, locally called tiff.

Two volcanos have been active recently. One is Soufriere in St. Vincent and the other is an underwater volcano off Isle de Ronde, north of Grenada. In addition, there are several active volcanic sites in the island chain, including steam and gas vents and the world's second largest boiling lake.

The once-molten core of the volcano is harder and more resistant to erosion than the surrounding material. Long after the softer cover gets washed away, the old volcano cores remain as spectacular sharp peaks, known as pitons. These, together with meandering streams in relatively

7

wide valleys, are signs of a mature topography. Islands of this type run from Saba to Basse-Terre in Guadeloupe and on down to Grenada.

The outlying flatter islands; Anguilla, St. Martins, St. Barts, Antigua, Barbuda, Guadeloupe's Grand Terre and Marie Galante, are much older. Originally they looked like the volcanic islands, but millions of years of erosion leveled them, including even the hard basaltic pitons. At some point, they eroded or subsided below sea level. Here they acquired a limestone capping. Later they were uplifted to their present positions.

Barbados alone is not volcanic. It is the top of a buckle in the seabed pushed above the surface when a tectonic plate got caught as it slid beneath another plate. The island was heavily capped in limestone during a later period when it was submerged.

On a geologic scale it was just yesterday, during the last ice age, that so much water was locked up as ice in glaciers that the sea level was about 300 feet lower than it is today. All species were able to freely migrate between islands without deep channels between them. Barbuda and Antigua were one, as were Grenada, the Grenadines and Bequia. Most islands, however, have never touched. There are channels over 4000 feet deep between St. Vincent and St. Lucia and between Dominica and Martinique. During the ice age islands provided larger targets for drifting seeds, plants and animals. All the life forms that colonized these islands have had to cross the sea. This was not hard for seabirds, and many land birds managed to fly up from South America. For land mammals it was more of a problem and anything too large to drift in on a raft of vegetation was excluded. Even today the islands do not have a very rich fauna. Ocean currents still bring seeds from the Canary Islands, the Mediterranean Basin, the coast of Africa and from the American mainland. Others are carried by birds. The lack of an easy exchange of seeds from continental land masses allowed the early plant colonizers to evolve into many different forms

and today many of the island plants and animals are unique to one island or to a small group of islands.

In temperate climes nature's rhythm is dominated by the seasons. Most of the year's ration of light and warmth comes in the summer months. The coming of spring is like the firing of a starting gun at a race track. Plants and animals take off for a period of frenzied activity which has to be completed before winter. Young must be raised and many plants have to grow, flower, and fruit in half a year.

The tropical climate of the Caribbean is far more constant. There is little difference in daylight hours or temperature throughout the year. Growing cycles are dictated instead by rainfall. Here there is a rainy season from about June to December and a drier season which is usually from January to May. These seasons are most pronounced at lower elevations, where many trees and shrubs lose their leaves. The low coastal hills turn a lovely pinkish brown when the vegetation sheds much of its surface area to preserve precious moisture. The beginning of the rainy season does have some of the excitement of a temperate spring. Seeds germinate and plants green up almost overnight.

The dry season, on the other hand, is ideal for flowering and pollination. Insects can move easily from flower to flower without getting whomped by monster raindrops and pollen is less likely to get washed away before it is delivered. It is during the dry season that most flowering plants explode into a riot of colorful blossoms.

Hurricanes are weather's wild cards. The usual hurricane season is from late June to early October. They strike, on average, about once in 20 years for any one place. But there can easily be two in as many years and then 50 years will pass before the next one hits. They are a significant factor in forest development, can totally wreck property and agricultural crops and occasionally they bring new plants and animals from afar. A hurricane bought locusts to St. Lucia in 1988 and a new orchid was found on Dominica not long after another storm. It may well have been a hurricane that first brought cattle egrets across the Atlantic.

The most dramatic changes to the ecology of the islands began with the arrival of humans. The Ciboneys may have been the first to reach the Caribbean islands, probably at about the time of Christ. They were soon followed by the Arawaks, in about 200 AD. The changes they brought, along with those of the Caribs who displaced them in about 1200 AD, were as nothing compared to what Europeans later did. But they are thought to have brought agoutis and manicous (opossums) as well as many plant species, including pineapples and anatto, a shrub whose seeds were used for body painting by Amerindians.

European influence began on a large scale in about 1650. The native vegetation was removed wherever possible and replaced by sugarcane. The work was done by slaves, the price of sugar was high and the profits made during the 200 years of sugar growing encouraged clearing and planting on a scale now hard to imagine. Antigua, for example, was planted in sugar almost to the tops of its peaks and almost no unaltered vegetation remains.

Along with the changes in plants came changes in the animal world as well. Eighty-seven vertebrate species are thought to have gone extinct in historic time. People have introduced many animals which have had a major impact on the local environment. Man's early imports included mice and at least four species of rats. The rats ate a lot of sugar and spoiled many times as much as they ate. To combat these pests, the Burmese mongoose was introduced to many islands. The mongoose, however, feeds by day and doesn't climb, so they didn't have much effect on the nimble nocturnal rats. Now rats eat the eggs of parrots and other tree-nesting birds and the mongoose eats native frogs, lizards, and the eggs and young of ground-nesting birds. Humans have also introduced domestic animals such as cats, dogs, goats and sheep. The monkeys of Grenada, St. Kitts and Nevis were introduced by Europeans and are not native. In Grenada, monkeys were probably responsible for the elimination of the local parrot.

Many islands have birds, lizards or plants that exist only on that one island. These endemic species, as they are called, are increasingly threatened. Conversion of forest to farmland to feed increasing populations and loss of habitat to other kinds of development are putting endemic species at risk of extinction. Nearly half the world's threatened birds are restricted to islands. There are now conservation groups on all the islands and each country is taking some steps to ensure that environmental issues are addressed in the development process.

This book is organized by habitat. Each area presents different opportunities and difficulties for its inhabitants. In dry coastal areas water is a limiting factor, and in the rain forest soils are poor and the competition for light is intense. We have tried to choose common and conspicuous species and to put each one in the environment where you are most likely to find it, but many plants and animals are not restricted to one habitat and some can make do anywhere.

Plants

1. White cedar
2. Beach pea
3. Madagascar periwinkle
4. Beach morning glory
5. Coconut
6. Casuarina
7. Manchineel
8. Indian almond
9. Seagrape

Birds

10. Magnificent frigatebird
11. Tropicbird
12. Brown pelican
13. Laughing gull
14. Royal tern
15. Brown booby
16. Osprey
17. Ruddy turnstone

Animals

18. Hawksbill turtle
19. Ghost crab
20. Sally lightfoot crab

Along the water's edge ghost crabs chase receding waves down the beach until they are in the very mouth of the next wave. They snatch tidbits that are exposed for only a fraction of a second, before making a dash for high ground. Sandpipers, too, walk the foaming edges of waves, high stepping like a group of fussy people trying to keep their shoes dry in wet grass.

Where the waves brush a sandy shore, the line between land and sea constantly shifts. For a time the land encroaches on the sea as sand is washed ashore and plants like beach morning glory and coconut trees send roots seaward to stabilize it. But the riches that the sea carelessly deposits are often as capriciously reclaimed. The twice daily high tides, the winter storm swells, or the hurricanes which arrive a few times each century are the sea's repo men, often taking away more than was given and sometimes washing away large trees, along with their hard-earned sand.

From a plant's point of view the beach is specialized real estate. Salt spray, relentless winds and shifting, nutrient-poor sand make survival difficult. But the sea deposits seeds, and those plants that overcome the difficulties are rewarded by plenty of light and little competition. Only a handful of plants are successful on the beach, so you will meet the same ones again and again throughout the region.

PLANTS

Coconut
Cocos nucifera

If you look up from your beach chair, chances are you will see a coconut tree. This unusual tree, like most other palms, has no branches; instead the leaves come right out of the trunk near the top. The trunk has no bark and no growth rings and does not get much thicker after it has formed for it has no cambium — the layer of dividing cells that encircles most tree trunks and makes them get wider and wider each year. As the tree pushes upwards, the lower leaves drop off and leave their marks all the way up the trunk. A baby coconut tree has large intact green leaves; as it grows bigger its leaves become enormous: 12 to 20 feet long. Hung out in the strong island winds, these would be like giant tearable sheets and so the older leaves are divided into long narrow segments. Hurricanes can remove the leaves of an adult tree, but the trunks are rarely toppled and soon leaf out again.

If you dig deeply in the sand behind the beach, you will come to salt water seeping in from the sea. When it rains, lighter fresh water forms a lens on top of the salt water. Coconut trees live on the fresh water from this lens. They can withstand an occasional flooding of salt water from a storm, but cannot survive indefinitely without rain. If you visit the islands during a long dry spell, you will notice the leaves folded downward. This greatly reduces water loss from evaporation and helps the coconut survive a drought.

The coconut tree is one of many palm species, and although palms are often seen on the sea shore and in the desert, there are also palms that grow in the rain forest. Palms are as old, or possibly older, than any other groups of flowering plants and the fruits of their Jurassic ancestors fattened early dinosaurs.

The coconut grows well in pure sand or in good soil, but you see it more often in the sand because in good soil other plants can grow faster and shade it out. Its natural habitat is a narrow band at the top of the beach. After the buoyant nuts are deposited, they can continue to inch up the beach as they grow, by reversing the usual order of germination. Most germinating seeds send roots out right away to anchor themselves, and then a green shoot emerges. In the coconut a tuft of leaves pokes out of the shell and begins photosynthesizing before any roots emerge. During this time the coconut is like a potted plant and can move up the beach on an extra high tide or large wave. Eventually, the coconut will begin to put out its thousands of small roots, which may extend 30 feet from the trunk.

The coconut tree produces an amazing seed, the second largest in the world, in a package which is harder to break into than those seamless plastic wrappings which encase nearly everything we buy these days. It has a tough but flexible outer green husk. Inside is a fibrous layer, a shock absorber that protects the inner nut, which, in turn, has an impervious brittle brown shell. It can sustain an 80-foot free-fall and is more waterproof and seaworthy than many a ship.

Coconuts originated in the western Pacific and eastern Indian Ocean and it was not until Portuguese explorers brought the nuts around Africa that they began colonizing the Atlantic Basin. The seed is adapted to endure long sea voyages and coconuts have found their own way to many islands, but their final destination is at the mercy of the currents. Maybe this is why Columbus made it across the Atlantic to the Caribbean before the coconut. Nowadays it is hard to think of a Caribbean beach without coconut palms, so it is surprising to discover that they are recent arrivals.

Almost every part of the coconut has been exploited and it is often called one of the most useful trees in the world. The leaves can be used as thatch or woven into mats and rope is made from the husks. Lumber is made from the trunks. Green coconuts yield a delicious drink and mature nuts contain a nutritious meat that can be eaten raw, made into coconut milk for cooking, or dried and used in hydraulic brake fluid, synthetic rubber or to produce soaps and cooking oils. The shells have been used to make a myriad of objects, some considerably more beautiful than others.

Beach morning glory
Ipomoea pes-caprae

If you take your eyes off the lofty coconut and look low on the beach where the vegetation begins, you may see the beach morning glory and the less common bay bean. Both flowering plants grow on tropical beaches around the world and are important as sand stabilizers. Beach morning glory seeds are dispersed by ocean currents and will sprout after being soaked in seawater

Beach morning glory

Coconut palm and seagrape, The Saintes

for up to six months. The plant, a vine with pink flowers, has thick, fleshy leaves on stiff, erect leaf stalks. The creeping stems, sometimes 30 feet long, strike out across the sand, edging nearer to the sea than any other plant. They make it almost to the edge of the high water mark, which is close to the sea indeed, as the tidal range in most of the islands is only a couple of feet. Beach morning glory's Latin name, *pes-caprae,* means "goat's foot" because if you flatten out a leaf (they are normally folded at the midrib), it has the shape of a goat's hoof.

One disadvantage of being a plant is that you cannot get up and move out of the way when attacked by a hungry insect or animal. The production of toxic compounds is a common plant tactic in the war against plant eaters. Beach morning glory protects its seeds and older leaves from predators by producing the poisonous alkaloid ergotamine (a chemical which is used for treating migraines, because it shrinks blood vessels).

After every move a plant makes on evolution's chessboard, however, the animal world gets to take a turn. Beetles in the genus *Megacerus* have evolved a method of breaking down ergotamine, and the female beetle lays an egg on a developing morning glory seed. The egg hatches into a larva which burrows into the seed, feeding as it goes and killing the embryo. But even these beetles appear to know which side their bread is buttered on. They are effective pollinators of the morning glory flowers and they don't lay eggs on every seed, ensuring that some seeds will develop normally. Both the beetle and the plant gain something from the relationship, which suggests that they have evolved together over a long time.

But poison is not the only way to protect against predators, and the young new leaves are protected by an army. The soldiers in this army are ants, and they are recruited by small nectar-secreting glands at the base of the plant's leaf stalks. These "extrafloral (outside the flower) nectaries" are a common phenomenon in tropical plants. They puzzled scientists at first.

Nectar in a flower we can understand, for it attracts pollinators; but why would a plant waste resources attracting insects to its leaves? It is because a bit of free food at the leaf bases attracts enough little soldiers to repel potential munchers of leaves and flower parts. The success of this ploy depends on the availability and willingness of the ants, but if you examine young beach morning glory leaves in a few locations, you are sure to find some six-legged recruits.

Bay bean
Canavalia roseus

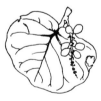

Bay bean is often intertwined with beach morning glory and superficially they look alike: both are long vines with pink flowers. But if you look closely you will see that the bay bean has a leaf with three leaflets and a typical pea flower.

Bay bean appears to have made its evolutionary move more recently. No insect has yet evolved with a mechanism to detoxify its poison, canavanine, and it is generally free of leaf or seed eaters.

Other names: seaside bean, beach pea.

Seagrape
Coccoloba uvifera

Between the low beach vines and the tall palms, you often find seagrapes. The seagrape is an adaptable plant, found both on calm leeward beaches and on low-lying eastern beaches that are exposed to the full force of the trade winds. Constant high winds prevent many trees from growing and they shape and prune those that do survive. If young tender shoots are blown over at an angle, the whole plant grows in a stunted, lopsided fashion. In these conditions the seagrape hugs the earth tightly, poking its branches just a small distance into the driven salt spray.

But given a protected beach on the leeward side of an island, seagrape reaches carelessly for the sky and becomes a full-blown tree, growing to 30 feet high. Here the round leaves may be six inches long and eight inches wide, in contrast to the three by four inch ones on windward shores. Seagrapes are in the same family (Polygonaceae) as buckwheat and have that family's insignia: a sheath that clasps the base of each petiole, or leaf stalk. The petioles are short (to half an inch). You may notice that some leaves are turned vertically, perhaps to decrease the amount of sunlight (and heat) that is intercepted. Usually plants work out ways to capture more light, but on a beach in the tropics something more like sunblock is called for.

Male and female flowers of the seagrape grow on separate plants. The flowers are borne on erect stalks and on the female plants edible grape-like fruits hang in clusters, turning from green to purple when ripe. They are on the sour side, but make good preserves. With a sharp pointed stick it is possible to write messages on the leaves and early Spanish colonists did this way back when paper was scarce, a condition which is hard to imagine today.

Indian almond, seaside almond
Terminalia catappa

You will often find the Indian almond tree close to the seagrapes. It is easy to recognize because its branches tend to grow in horizontal layers. Its large dark green leaves (six to eleven inches long) are widest near the tip and are bunched together at the ends of the twigs. Old leaves turn bright red before they are shed.

This tree is not related to the familiar food item. It was introduced from India and has been widely planted in the American tropics. The Indian almond repays people for their efforts by providing dense shade on the beach and being tolerant of both salt spray and pure sand. It also grows fast, has edible fruits and useful wood, produces tannins which have been used for tanning leather, and an oil has been extracted from the fruits.

The tiny white flowers are clustered around a central stalk. The fruits are about one inch wide and two inches long, somewhat flattened, with noticeable edges. You may want to eat some out of curiosity, as the nuts are something like the almond you are more familiar with. But the effort of extracting them is likely to prevent you from putting chicken amandine on the menu, unless you are stranded on a beach with a rock and a hammer and have finished your detective novel.

Manchineel
Hippomane mancinella

Don't try to eat the fruit of the manchineel and don't touch it so roughly that you get sap on your skin! Manchineel is so toxic that the sap was used by the Caribs to poison their arrows, and so caustic it can take the paint off a car.

"*Hippomane*" means horse poison. If there is just one tree you should learn to recognize in the Caribbean, it is the pretty manchineel tree which grows along many beaches. Once you know it, you can avoid its toxins and will not need to look warily at every tree on the beach. None but the manchineel poses a real hazard.

Manchineels grow to be 40 feet high and over two feet in diameter, although most are much smaller. The branches fork widely, giving a generous spread-out shape to the tree. The shiny dark green elliptic leaves are often folded at the midrib and have long yellowish leaf stalks. The leaves have a droopy appearance, much like those on a common pear tree. If you look closely at the junction of leaf and leaf stalk, you will see a tiny raised dot, about the size of a pin head. This is a gland and it will help you identify the manchineel, the only beach tree which has this feature.

The fruits are attractive, shiny green, and look like little apples. They are reported to taste quite good, but they are very

Nesting frigatebirds, Barbuda

poisonous. It is the apples and the milky sap of manchineel which cause problems, and both can be avoided. Milky sap escapes whenever a leaf or branch is injured. It can cause severe blistering of the skin and even a minute quantity, if gotten in the eyes, can be very painful and cause at least temporary blindness. So avoid getting scratched by the tree, do not break off branches or sit on freshly fallen leaves. Smoke from burning branches can be highly irritating, so this is not a good choice for your beachside barbecue. It is unwise to shelter under a manchineel tree in the rain, as latex from small everyday wounds may get washed onto you with the drips. Should you run afoul of a manchineel, the best immediate first aid is probably a thorough washing in the sea.

Many plants count on mammals or birds to eat their fruits and then deposit the seeds (complete with fertilizer) at a site some distance from the parent plant. Only land crabs are immune to manchineel's toxins and they perform this function. The apples also float and many are dispersed by the sea. Manchineels are nearly always found close to the beach, though once in a while one will find its way inland.

Manchineels are common native trees and add beauty and shade to many beaches. There are no reports of manchineels reaching out and hitting anyone over the head. In parts of Puerto Rico and Florida, they have been nearly eradicated, which seems unnecessarily destructive. The French often mark the trees with a scull and crossbones warning. In the other islands you should learn to recognize them for yourself. Once you know about manchineels, they pose little threat.

White cedar
Tabebuia heterophylla

White cedar, sometimes known as West Indies cedar is often found on the beach. Despite its name, this tropical tree has nothing in common with northern white cedar (*Thuja occidentalis*) which is found in the northeastern US and eastern Canada.

White cedar trees grow inland, as well as on the beach. They can grow on soil that has been severely de-

18

graded by cultivation and has become similar to beach sand in moisture holding capacity and nutrient content. Like seagrapes they are adaptable and may be large trees or tiny plants, depending on the environment. At their best they are glorious, growing to 60 feet high, with straight trunks and narrow columnar crowns. Showy, fragrant tubular pink flowers, about two and half inches long, are abundant in the early spring and occur in smaller numbers throughout the year. The seed pods look like thin dangling cigars, brown when mature and green while developing.

The species name, "*heterophylla*," refers to the occurrence of "different leaves" on these trees. Some leaves are simple leaves, others are compound leaves with up to five leaflets radiating from a point. In some areas, all the trees have only simple leaves. In any event, the leaflets or leaves are elliptic, shiny, and blunt at both the tip and the base. They are light green when young and darker green later. The wood is widely used in the islands for boat building and is excellent for cabinet work, being both beautiful and easy to work.

Casuarina
Casuarina equisetifolia

The casuarina tree, sometimes known as Australian pine, is an introduced tree with long drooping branches, originally from tropical Asia and Australia. It does very well on protected leeward beaches, but it has not been as successful at colonizing new beaches in the Caribbean as coconut palms or Indian almonds. It is frequently planted, especially near hotels, because it is pretty, fast growing and useful as a windbreak. Its pine-like "needles," which grow to about 18 inches long, are really branches; the true leaves are colorless scales, only one 32nd of an inch long. In this tree the branches do the photosynthesizing and as they get old, they turn gray-brown and fall off, much as a more typical tree sheds leaves.

Male and female flowers grow on the same tree and the fruit is a warty light brown cone-like ball, a bit like a tiny pineapple.

White cedar

Madagascar periwinkle
Catharanthus roseus

You will often see Madagascar periwinkles, which are native to Madagascar, around hotels. These cheerful perennials grow well in sand. They are planted for their bright pink or white five-petalled flowers which are produced in small clusters at the tips of the branches. They protect themselves with vincristine and vinblastine, two toxic alkaloids which kill actively dividing cells. These have been extracted and used in the chemotherapeutic treatment of human leukemias.

Periwinkles are not only pretty. They are tough and have found their own way around to barren waste areas, as well as to the upper edges of the beach.

BIRDS

Magnificent frigatebird
Fregata magnificens

Fish and the birds that feed on them are drawn to the shallow, rich waters just off the beach. Here the bird watcher doesn't have to contend with a mess of similar-looking tiny birds that disappear into the bushes just as the binoculars are lifted to the face. Many birds in this habitat are large and easy to recognize.

If you look high in the distance you will often see long-winged black birds, riding the wind. This is typical behavior for the magnificent frigatebird, sometimes called the man o'war bird.

This bird is common and unmistakable. Black, with a lethal looking, sharply hooked bill, a deeply forked tail, and large pointed wings bent at the wrist, it looks distinctly prehistoric. The forked tail can be opened and closed like scissors, and in patois the name of this bird is "siso." The males have a strip of pinkish skin on the throat which is blown up like a bright red balloon when it is time to impress a female. Females have white breasts and sides, and the immatures of both sexes have white heads and breasts.

Weighing just two to three pounds and with a wingspan of seven to eight feet, frigatebirds have a lower ratio of weight to wing area than any other bird. They soar effortlessly, rarely alighting except at the nest site or to roost for the night. However, this evolution toward aerial excellence is not without cost, for frigatebirds have wettable feathers and cannot take off from water, so a crash landing could be fatal. In addition, they are bumblers on land. They need consistent wind at the nest site to get airborne.

They can catch fish at the surface of the water, but, because they are unable to dive, they probably could not survive on this source alone. To make ends meet they have become pirates of the air. They use their long beaks and superb flying skills to harass other birds, chasing them until they drop their catch, which is then swooped up in midair. It is for their agility and these marauding habits that they got their names. Frigatebirds are quarrelsome among themselves as well as against their neighbors, which sometimes makes for a spectacular avian airshow.

Frigatebirds have been used by Polynesians as homing pigeons, carrying messages to tell that sailors had safely arrived at a distant island.

They nest in colonies and during the mating season the male brings some sticks for a nest to a suitable bush, sits on them, inflates his incredible scarlet throat pouch, and cackles hoarsely. If all goes well, a female is entranced, builds the nest, and lays one large egg. It takes 55 days to hatch and the nestling is fed for about six months by both parents before it can fly and leave the nest. After this it continues to be fed, mostly by the mother, for up to 14 months more. This is among the longest periods of dependency known for any bird. The largest frigatebird colony in the Lesser Antilles is in Codrington Lagoon in Barbuda. In the breeding season the mangroves are peppered with nests, spread with guano, and hundreds of squawking birds, the males with their red throat sacs dangling like balloons, fill the air.

Brown booby
Sula leucogaster

Brown boobies are often chased and robbed by frigatebirds. The name "booby" is from the Spanish "bobo," or dunce, as at one time it was easy for hungry sailors to approach these birds and grab them for food. Now the survivors tend to nest in remote inaccessible areas.

Boobies are large birds, about 27 inches long, and are streamlined and pointed at both ends. The brown booby is the most common of the three booby species in the Caribbean and is often seen in a group, flying so close to the water that its wings narrowly miss the wave tops. All the feathers are brown, except on the snowy white breast and under the inner part of the wings which is also white. The feet and bill are yellow. The bill is broad at the base, and sometimes has a pink or greenish tinge.

Boobies love fish, especially flying fish, and they are excellent fishermen. They plunge-dive under the surface and chase their prey underwater, sometimes for as long as 40 seconds. Generally they dine alone, but they congregate at concentrations of fish.

Brown Pelican
Pelicanus occidentalis

There is no need to describe the pelican. He is well known to all limerick readers: "A wonderful bird is the pelican. His bill can hold more than his belly can." And his belly can hold quite a bit, for these are large birds. With a wingspan of six and half to seven and a half feet, they tip the scales at up to eight pounds, and yet a dried skeleton weighs only nine ounces. The enormous pouch is used as a dip net and can contain a couple of gallons of water as well as fish. Contrary to popular belief, the pouch is not used to carry fish. This is done in the esophagus.

Pelicans have superb control in the air. It is hard to believe they are the same birds that bring condescending smiles when seen waddling along a dock. They fly to their fishing grounds in single file and with coordinated wing strokes, with their heads tucked back and their long bills resting on their necks. There they glide without flapping their wings until fish are sighted. Then a pelican will tuck in its wings and make a spectacular plunge. At this point art vanishes and comedy begins as a tangled mess of wings and an unmanageably full pouch bob to the surface. The excess water is messily expelled, the fish swallowed with rude gulps, and the laborious process of becoming airborne begins. The bird beats its big wings and pounds the surface with both feet in unison. For a few seconds it looks hopeless. Then the great splashing about ends and gracefulness returns.

If you've ever done a bellyflop you may wonder how the pelican can free fall from a great height and make such a whopping splash without hurting itself. The answer is that the pelican is equipped with nature's version of the air bags in modern cars. Birds have additional air chambers connected to the lungs which ventilate the body and help keep them cool. In pelicans and boobies, the air chambers also act as shock absorbers and cushion their dives. They also provide buoyancy.

Pelicans nest in colonies and nest spacing is determined by the distance that a sitting bird can stretch its neck toward its neighbors. The parents take turns sitting on the two to four eggs, pecking at the neighbors, and feeding the young.

Laughing gull
Larus atricilla

The seagull you are most likely to see is the laughing gull, the only breeding gull in the Lesser Antilles. It is a pretty bird, small for a gull: about 16 inches long, compared to the 24 inch herring gull that some might be familiar with. Laughing gulls often hang out on sand spits, seldom venture far offshore, and feed on fish, shrimp, and crabs along with scraps from fishing boats, dead small animals and offal. A laughing gull's call is an excited "ha, ha, ha, ha." If you throw bread for them, they will sometimes come.

Though the laughing gull is very distinctive in the breeding season, from April to July, with red legs and bill, black wing tips, and a chocolate-dipped head resting on a snow white neck, it is less memorable in winter and in the immature stages. At these times its dramatic black head is replaced with a mere shadow of a hood, the bill is dusky, the legs blackish. Immature birds have a dark band across the top of the tail and lack the black wing tips. Young gulls take several years to develop adult plumage. Most laughing gulls go to the north coast of Venezuela for the winter, returning in early April to breed.

Laughing gulls nest on remote rocky cliffs. Two or three spotted eggs are laid in a rough nest, par for the course among seabirds. The male guards the female while she incubates the eggs and helps care for the nestlings.

Royal tern
Sterna maxima

The bird you are most likely to confuse the laughing gull with is the royal tern. Gulls and terns are cousins, seabirds in the same family, the Laridae. On the gull side, however, you will notice stout slightly hooked bills which go with their omnivorous scavenging ways, whereas the tern side of the family has slender sharp-pointed bills, useful in the fish catching business. Gulls have longish legs and walk about, while terns have short legs and are disinclined to walk. Gulls also tend to have broader wings and rounder tails. The laughing gull and the royal tern are quite common on most small Caribbean islands. Both have been seen sitting on pelicans' heads snatching food from the pouch. In turn, laughing gulls and royal terns are often the targets of frigatebird robberies.

Most gulls are larger than most terns but the laughing gull is small as gulls go and the royal tern is large as terns go; at 19 inches long, the royal tern is one of the largest, even a little larger than the laughing gull, though from a distance they look about the same size.

The royal tern has a yellow or orange bill, white undersides, gray wings, black feet and a black crest which is striking in the breeding season. Out of season the black crest is just a small mottled area at the

Ghost crab

22

back of the head. Like most terns, royal terns make their living by fishing. They plunge-dive, often from considerable heights. When not at work they can be seen sitting on exposed coral heads, sand spits, or salt pond dikes.

White-tailed tropicbirds
Phaethon lepturus
Red-billed tropicbirds
P. aethereus

It is easy to recognize tropicbirds because of their wonderful long tail streamers. About half the length of the adults is in tail feathers. They feed far out at sea in summer and fall, without seeing land for months at a time, but return to nest in holes in rocky cliffs from December to June. If you like to hike around cliffs you will probably see them near their nests. Their short webbed feet are inadequate for walking and they much prefer to be able to jump from their nests without having to walk. They live on flying fish and squid, caught by diving.

There are two species of tropicbirds in the Caribbean, both beautiful. Both are basically white. The white-tailed is more common and has a yellow bill and a solid black band across its wing. The red-billed has delicate black barring on its wings.

Other name: boatswain's bird.

Osprey, sea eagle
Pandion haliaetus

If you are lucky, you may see what is obviously a bird of prey hanging like a kite over the water or perched high in a tree. Chances are this is an osprey, a bird which is distributed world-wide. Almost the size of eagles, ospreys live exclusively on fish, which they catch in their talons after diving feet first into the water. If you are really lucky and see one catch a fish, watch it turn the fish and carry it head first to reduce windage. Ospreys have white heads and underparts and brown backs. They can travel long distances; an osprey shot in Barbuda was found to have been ringed as a fledgling in Greenland some six months before.

Sandpipers

Without question, the gregarious little brown and white wading birds that scurry along the beach in flocks are difficult to identify. At least 12 sandpiper species occur in the Lesser Antilles, and six of these can be found on almost every island. Sandpipers are land bound, but most feed from water. They spend their time right where the waves wash the shore, grabbing a wide variety of animals and even some plants. The shoreline ranges from rocks to sand to mud and this diversity attracts many different bird species.

Ruddy turnstones *(Arenaria interpres)* are the easiest to identify. These plump little shorebirds have short necks and orange legs. In flight turnstones show a striking pattern on their backs and wings, with bold contrasting areas of black, white and reddish brown. They congregate on rocky or sandy shores or mudflats where they do, indeed, turn stones over, along with shells and debris, to look for mollusks, crustaceans, fish eggs and vegetable matter.

Unlike the turnstones, the names of sandpipers are not helpful in sorting out who's who. The spotted sandpiper *(Actitus macularia)* only has spots during its brief breeding season. It bobs its tail when walking or just standing and often you will just see one, not a flock.

Two sandpipers, the semipalmated *(Calidris pusilla)* and western *(Calidrus mauri)* sandpipers, are found in the same areas. Both avoid rocky areas and frequent gently sloping or flat, sandy, mud or gravel shores, but the two species have separate and characteristic feeding strategies. The western is considerably more active, running briskly, and pecking as rapidly as a sewing machine. Semipalmateds do less probing as they forage for creatures near or on the surface.

The solitary sandpiper *(Tringa solitaria)* is solitary only part of the time, though if it is in a flock, it's a loose one. Solitaries prefer fresh water, especially areas where the vegetation comes nearly to the water's edge. There, with bobbing heads and tilting bodies, they probe for aquatic insects, small mollusks and crustaceans.

The pectoral sandpiper *(Calidrus melanotos)* is found along lagoons and wet meadows, feeding in vegetation a bit away from the water.

Having put all these different sandpipers into neat categories by habitat and feeding behavior, we must now admit that many flocks will contain more than one species of sandpiper. A bird book such as "Birds of the West Indies," by James Bond, or "Birds of the Eastern Caribbean" by Peter Evans will help you sort out the different species.

Ghost crab
Ocypode quadrata

Crisscrossing the sandpiper tracks, you can often see a zigzag meshwork of crab tracks, usually ending in a burrow just above the high tide line. These were probably made by the ghost crab, an animal whose common and scientific names each contain a clue to its identification. It mimics the light-colored sand on which it lives so well that it has a ghostly air. One minute you see it, the next it is gone. And the generic name, *Ocypode*, means "swift footed," another notable feature of this animal, which can dash across the sand so fast that it is almost impossible to catch, even if it can't find a burrow.

The ghost crab has a squarish carapace with a H-shaped depression in the center, long legs, and long eye stalks. There are 11 *Ocypode* species world-wide, but only one in the western Atlantic.

These active crabs are keen predators. They snack on beach fleas, small dark crustaceans which live beneath seaweed, and other debris at the high tide line. They also dig in wet sand at the edges of waves and pounce on mole crabs and tiny mollusks. Ghost crabs are basically nocturnal and those you see out at midday are having what for us would be a midnight snack. For each crab you see, there are many others tucked safely in their burrows. If you stop and sit quietly on your moonlight walk on the beach, you may find yourself in the midst of crab rush hour.

This is the first of several land crabs we will meet. These animals are of great interest to biologists, partly because they are in the midst of an evolutionary transition; moving from the sea onto dry land. Oxygen is 40 to 60 times more available in air than in water and the ghost crab assimilates it by absorption under its shell. The ghost crab still has some gills, but they are far smaller than those of marine crabs and it will drown if submerged for an extended period.

These creatures could be said to be between the devil and the deep blue sea for, in addition to the danger of drowning, they will die if their gills are not kept moist. Though the gills are not used to get oxygen, they do perform other functions, such as getting rid of carbon dioxide and regulating blood volume and composition. Gills need water to function and land crabs have made behavioral, structural, and physiological adaptations to stay wet. Ghost crabs have special tufts of hair which can extract moisture from sand which contains as little as five percent water. They generally spend the heat of the day in damp burrows and can sometimes be seen making quick forays into the water to wet their gills.

It appears that ghost crabs do not enjoy digging their three foot long burrows. A large ghost crab will enter an undersized burrow and then back out, allowing the smaller occupant to escape. It will then enlarge the burrow and make itself at home. The displaced crab goes on to steal a smaller burrow from a smaller crab, and so goes the game of musical burrows, until the smallest crabs have to start digging afresh.

Scientists call crabs decapods because they have ten legs. One pair of legs, the pincers, is not used for walking, but serves as what most would call arms: appendages used for gesturing to other crabs and picking up food. Many crabs, including ghost crabs, walk sideways which can appear quite comical, especially when the crabs change direction to give the trailing legs, which do the pushing, a rest. But if we had eight walking legs, we, too, might find this method the best for keeping them from getting tangled up in each other.

Sally lightfoot crab
Grapsus grapsus

These dark crabs with almost circular shells spend most of their time on land, but never stray more than a foot or two from the sea. You can find them on rocks and docks within the splash zone. They are easy to see from a distance, but as you approach, they scurry into the safety of the water or a crack in the rocks. They are land crabs, but can still spend considerable time under water, keeping, as it were, five feet in each environment.

They will eat almost anything and can run fast enough to catch it. Their courtship includes a complex dancing pattern.

Sea turtles

There are 250 species of turtles, but only eight are sea turtles. All of the sea turtles commonly found in the Caribbean are endangered species, but on a charmed evening you may see a female sea turtle haul herself up the beach to lay eggs, an enterprise fraught with danger, both for the mother and the little ones. Nesting ashore is a holdover from the distant past when sea turtles lived on land.

The eggs incubate in the sand for nearly two months and the little turtles usually emerge at night - avoiding the frigatebirds, but not the patrolling night herons.

It takes decades for sea turtles to grow from tiny hatchlings, the size of a child's hand, to the size at which they begin reproducing. A female green turtle, for example, will be from 20 to 50 years old when she lays her first eggs. Turtle hatchlings use the earth's magnetic field, along with other clues from the environment, such as the direction of the waves, to reach the Sargasso Sea. They ride the circling currents of this vast area for several years before adopting the foraging style of their parents. After reaching a predator-resistant size, the growing turtles head toward shore. Adult turtles, except leatherbacks, tend to feed from the bottom and 300 feet is their diving limit.

Hawksbills (*Eretmochelys imbricata*) forage around reefs and the primary food of the adults is sponges. Other encrusting organisms round out the diet. Adult green turtles (*Chelonia mydas*) eat seagrasses. Loggerheads (*Caretta caretta*) eat such things as crabs and clams. Leatherbacks (*Dermochelys coriacea*), the largest of all sea turtles, forage far from land and mostly subsist on jellyfish. Many have been killed because they eat discarded plastic bags. These look like jellyfish, but hopelessly clog the turtle's intestines.

Some turtles use just a few beaches for nesting which makes it possible to protect them by turning those beaches into refuges. This doesn't work for hawksbills which nest singly on any beach. A tagging project which began in 1987 at Long Island, off Antigua, has revealed that the hawksbills begin nesting in early May and continue through November. The females nest up to five times and an average of 157 eggs is laid each time. They don't nest again for several years.

Most turtles are hunted for their flesh. The leatherback is considered unpalatable, but the females are sometimes taken for their eggs. Hawksbill turtles have the most beautiful shells and this, as well as their edible flesh, has gotten them into trouble. Many islands now regulate the taking of turtles. If the trade in tortoiseshell could be stopped, it might give the hawksbills a chance. More tourists are taking an interest in turtles and sometimes join in turtle watches organized by local conservation organizations. If live turtles, rather than turtle soup or turtle shell are recognized as tourist attractions, this will lessen their peril.

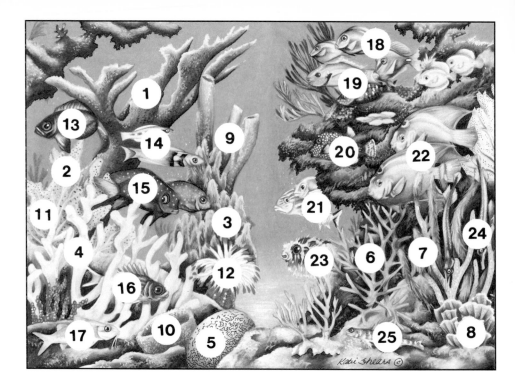

Corals

1. Elkhorn
2. Sea fan
3. Pillar coral
4. Finger coral
5. Brain coral
6. Staghorn
7. Deadman's fingers
   (Gorgonian soft coral)
8. Fire coral

Sponges

9. Yellow tube sponge
10. Vase sponge

Mollusk

11. Flamingo tongue

Anemone

12. Giant Caribbean anemone

Fish

13. Bigeye
14. Bluehead wrasse
    (includes terminal male)
15. Yellowtail damselfish
16. Squirrelfish
17. Goatfish
18. Blue tangs
    (includes 2 yellow immatures)
19. Stoplight parrotfish
    (includes terminal male)
20. Boxfish
21. French grunts
22. Queen angelfish
23. Pufferfish
24. Trumpetfish
25. Sand diver

Sitting in a boat, anchored next to a reef, the rippling waves and the shore beyond are reassuringly familiar. But put on a mask and slip into the water and you will find yourself in a world as alien as a distant planet.

You may see ancient-looking urns, glowing an eerie shade of blue. These are sponges, as are the bright yellow clumps of tubes nearby. An incredible variety of brightly colored fish allow you to swim quite near them - unlike the birds you may have tried to watch on land. It is an Alice-in-Wonderland world where nothing is quite as it seems. Solid-looking boulders turn out to be colonies of tiny animals, as do tall waving "plants."

Because we have to walk to the kitchen to get a sandwich, it is hard for us to imagine animals that spend all of their adult lives rooted in one spot, like trees, unable to move. Even if our feet were glued to the floor in a well-stocked kitchen, we would soon consume the food within reach and die of starvation. But water is a heavier medium than air and it carries an array of small vegetable and animal life, called plankton. This dilute organic soup flows along at the mercy of the currents and feeds the rooted animals. The organisms of a large healthy reef trap nearly all the plankton that floats by them and transform it into a complex and flourishing ecosystem: an island of life within an otherwise sparsely populated sea.

Away from the tropics, the surface of the water is colder than the bottom waters and the warmer bottom water rises, bringing nutrients up from the seabed. This feeds the cold water plankton which thrives in the sunlit upper levels of the sea. Plankton is the basis of a food chain which supports the majority of the world's fish, and fuels even mighty whales. In colder regions plankton is so abundant that the water is murky. Tropical seas are far clearer. Here the surface water is warm year round and the waste products that sink to the bottom stay there. Nutrients are scarce and plankton is not plentiful. Marine life is spread thinly - except on the coral reef.

The reef food chain begins, as in all ecosystems, with plants which convert sunlight and nutrients into vegetable matter. Some of this plant matter consists of tiny free floating plants (the phytoplankton) which feed minute crustaceans and other animals (the zooplankton). These in turn get eaten by fish, which get eaten by larger fish. Another major source of food is the algae which grow on any suitable hard surface. Dead coral provides an excellent surface for algae to grow on and it is closely grazed by many reef fish. Other plant matter grows inside the coral polyps. Coral does not make an easy lunch. As we shall see, it has some good defenses, but urchins, crabs, snails and some fish do manage to consume it.

The most important contribution of coral is to provide shelter or a firm anchoring spot for thousands of species of fish and invertebrates. The small coral polyps, most less than an inch in diameter, and sometimes so small that there are 250 of them per square inch, can create an impressive edifice: some Caribbean reefs contain several times the building material that exists in New York City. Built over thousands of years, they are the products of countless generations of coral polyps.

HARD CORALS

A coral reef begins with a minute free-floating larva of a coral polyp. It drifts for a while, part of the moving plankton. Most of its siblings get eaten, but one in a million finds its way to a new home. It cannot stop just anywhere; it needs a hard surface in clean water on which to grow. Once established, the free floating stage turns into a polyp, the basic building block of a coral reef. The polyp is basically a stomach from which

Flower coral (a hard coral), with polyps extended

tentacles reach out to trap passing plankton. Coral tentacles carry such an awesome arsenal of weapons that they could have been created by a writer of horror movies. Along the tentacles are knobbly areas of special cells (cnidoblasts) which, when triggered, cause coiled threads (nematocysts) to explode out of the cells. Some of these threads are whiplike and coil round the plankton, grabbing it. Some are coated with sticky mucous which acts like aggressive fly paper. Others contain barbs and paralyzing poisons.

When the tiny coral larva was cast adrift by its parents, they equipped it with a gift -- a few cells of a yellow-brown algae called zooxanthellae. These plants are crucial to the coral's success. Though coral traps most passing plankton, this provides only 6 to 13% of the food necessary to produce a reef. The rest is made inside the coral by the zooxanthellae which live in the polyp's stomach. Like most other plants, these algae need sunlight and if

corals often look like plants, it is no accident: both are doing their best to maximize exposure to the light. If a patch of coral is covered with something that cuts out the light, the zooxanthellae die and their coral hosts soon follow. Light is unable to penetrate very deeply into the sea, so all large living reef structures are within about 170 feet of the surface. Below that some corals can grow without zooxanthellae, but only very slowly.

Coral waste products fertilize the zooxanthellae and the coral provides it with a refuge from predators and a place in the sun. In return, the zooxanthellae provide nutrients for the coral and reduce the acid level in the polyps, enabling the coral to produce its calcium skeletons much faster than it could without these live-in plants.

The polyp makes itself a coat of armor by excreting calcium carbonate to form a rock-hard wall. This is firmly cemented to those of its neighbors. (Calcium is readily available from seawater.) Once estab-

Yellow tube sponge, with a damselfish

31

lished, the coral starts to reproduce by sending out new buds which grow up next door, and as each of these sends out more new buds, so the reef grows. Coral polyps grow in huge colonies, new generations growing on top of the old, until they create a wall extending from the sea bed to the surface, stretching for miles at a time. Each new polyp is a separate animal, capable of surviving on its own, but it retains stomach links to its parent and its children so the whole colony can share food, and to some extent, act in unison.

If you swim up to a piece of coral you will see that the surface is covered with a repetitive pattern. Often the pattern is an array of disks, where each disk is one coral polyp. Sometimes, as with brain corals, you will notice long groove-like patterns. These corals grow sideways until they get so long they split themselves into two. In this way they form long chains of polyps. Like row houses, they share side walls with their neighbors, but each has its own front and back wall.

Dividing into two, time and time again, is a fast, safe, and sure way to bring forth the new family members necessary for building a reef. But each new little polyp is the spitting image of her mother, with all her strengths and weaknesses. Once established, corals also reproduce sexually, pushing out their seed with currents made by beating tiny hairs (cilia). Sexual reproduction, although complicated, is beneficial because the mixing of genes allows for the creation of new characteristics. These oddballs may be able to meet new challenges.

Life forms evolve to take advantage of any resource that is not fully exploited by an already existing species. On the reef corals come in a myriad of shapes and sizes, each a specialist in its own way. Two conflicting requirements -- for a large surface area and for resistance to sea action -- give rise to some ingenious architectural solutions. Added to this dilemma is the fact that areas of hard bottom, needed for the coral's foundation, are scarce. Once anchored, it is an advantage to be able to spread out over a large area from a small base. Elkhorn coral's *(Acropora palmata)* solution is to flatten its branches to present a broad surface to the sun and a cutting edge to the waves. By doing so, it can stand tall in rough conditions. If you examine a large area with several kinds of coral, you will find many approaches to solving this problem. This results in a complex and convoluted structure which inadvertently creates passages, pillars, chambers and grottos at many levels.

Staghorn *(Acropora cervicornis)*, elkhorn, and brain corals (such as depressed brain coral *Diploria labyrinthiformis*), tend to feed at night, so you do not see their tentacles in the daytime. However, should you brush against one by mistake, you will feel the slimy mucous put out to snare passing prey. Pillar coral *(Dendrogyra cylindrus)* and finger corals (in the genus *Porites*) have their fuzzy tentacles extended during the day, and if gently touched, they will withdraw. Sometimes one small touch will cause the whole coral structure to withdraw after a few seconds, showing that each coral polyp is communicating with the next.

FIRE CORALS

 Although corals are lethal to plankton, most won't affect a snorkeler. However, one group of corals packs a punch so strong they will cause a rash if you brush against them, and they should be avoided. These are fire corals. Fire corals are smooth and don't have coral cups; instead the polyps show as tiny pinholes on the surface. They are often a bright yellow-beige color with whitish tips. Flat-topped fire coral *(Millepora complanata)* often grows in profusion on a fringing reef, right

where the waves break over it. Crenelated fire coral (*Millepora alcicornis*) forms branches and can be common in the shallows, growing on dead coral, wrecks and docks.

SOFT CORALS

Among the hard corals you will find soft corals: seafans, forked sea feathers (*Psuedopterogorgia bipinnata*), deadman's fingers *(Briareum asbestinum)*, spiny candelabra *(Muricea muricata)*, tan bushy soft coral *(Plexaura flexuosa)* and other creatures that look so much like plants that they could have been placed there by an interior decorator as the finishing touch. These corals are mainly of the gorgonian family. Like the hard corals, soft corals are colonies of polyps, but their skeletons consist of needles of calcium carbonate, encased in a softer, more flexible material. Because they feed during the day they don't directly compete with the night-feeding hard corals. Soft corals can live on next to nothing and are often abundant in sheltered places that do not get continually washed with fresh plankton. Many have a soft, bushy outer layer. If you look closely, you can see that this consists of tentacles extending from small holes. Sea fans are always oriented crosswise to the current to offer the maximum surface area to the passing water. A glance can tell you which way the current runs.

ENEMIES OF CORAL

There are about 700 species of coral in the Indo-Pacific reef system and only about 40 species in the Caribbean. This makes the Caribbean corals more vulnerable to a catastrophe. Corals only live in water which is consistently above 68° F. They thrive within a narrow temperature range and recently there has been speculation that rising water temperatures, caused by global warming, may be contributing to coral loss. In 1987 and 1990, zooxanthellae died throughout the Caribbean, and the loss of these brown algae left the coral looking whiter than normal. This phenomenon is called "coral bleaching" and the reasons for the death and recovery are not known.

Although some corals can clean themselves of silt by creating currents with their cilia, many are destroyed by this form of pollution. Some dead coral that you see is a natural part of the reef; other coral may have been destroyed by silt from building projects or by run-off or chemicals from poorly managed agriculture.

The lives of reef organisms revolve around nutrients and it is a lucky bit of plankton, indeed, that makes it across a reef without being consumed by some creature. You might think that nutrient rich run-off containing fertilizers or sewage would enrich the hungry reef. But reefs flourish not in spite of low nutrient levels, but because of them. The macro-algae, which we know as seaweeds, require high nutrient levels. If excess nutrients reach the reef, it can be quickly overgrown with seaweed, cutting out light to coral and obliterating the delicate balance which exists between reef organisms.

FLAMINGO TONGUE

If you look closely at seafans (*Gorgonia ventalina*), you will soon see the beautiful flamingo tongue (*Cyphoma gibbosum*). This little mollusk eats the seafan, and you may see a trail of dead seafan behind it. If there are only one or two on a seafan, the trail will not be very long. The seafan can reproduce itself fast

Squirrelfish (blackbar soldierfish) resting by day

enough to keep up, and no permanent damage is done. Don't be tempted to collect this little fellow, for his pretty outlined orange spots are part of his soft and perishable mantle, not marks on the shell. (The mantle is the mollusk's retractable "skin;" a thin fleshy membrane which secretes materials for the hard calcareous shell.)

SEA ANEMONES

Sea anemones were named because of their resemblance to the pretty terrestrial flowers, but the likeness ends with appearances. Sea anemones are animals which grow to more than a foot in diameter and they are as well armed as their coral relatives. Some capture fish, mollusks and sea stars and others feed on tiny floating animals, but all can sting, poison and paralyze their prey. Many have zooxanthellae living within their tentacles.

The giant Caribbean anemone (*Condylactis gigantea*) damages coral by sitting on it. Look for cleaning shrimps or small fish taking refuge among its thick six inch long purple-tipped light-colored tentacles. Over 30 species of reef fish have been seen seeking protection among anemone tentacles, and why they are not eaten by their host is something of a puzzle. Anemones are usually well-anchored but they can shuffle slowly from place to place. For most anemones the trip is a slow one, but one species, the tricolor anemone, is often picked up by a hermit crab and carried on its shell for protection, a symbiotic relationship which introduces the anemone to more food than it would find on its own.

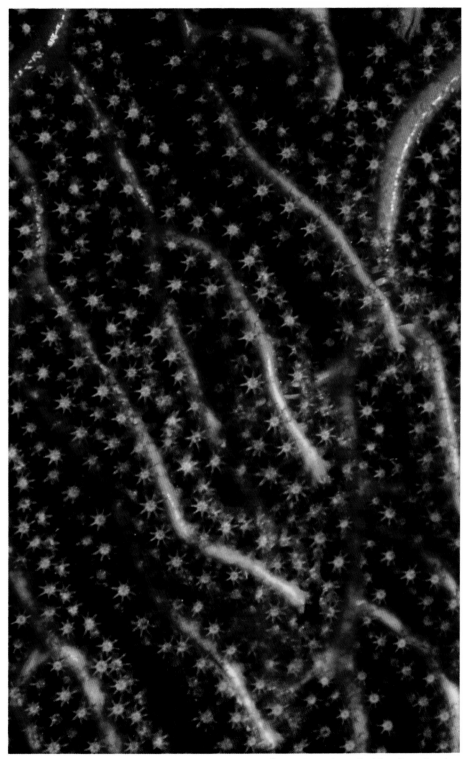

Gorgonian soft coral with polyps showing

One fascinating underwater phenomenon is the cleaning station, an area on the reef where larger fish are cleaned of parasites and dead tissue by smaller cleaning fish or by shrimps. Several fish species do cleaning, some part time and some full time. Cleaning gobies and some shrimps are the easiest to spot. The cleaners set up shop, hanging out together, often on top of a coral boulder. Soon they get visited by fish. Sometimes the demand for their services is so great that the fish line up. The larger fish have various ways of signaling to the shrimps that they have come to be cleaned and not to dine. This is important because many of these fish would find a shrimp or small fish a tasty morsel. Apparently, the evolutionary value of having the cleaners remove parasites and dead skin is so great that a truce has evolved. If you find an empty cleaning station where the attendants are shrimps, approach very slowly and place your outstretched hand, knuckle side up in front of a shrimp. Sometimes it will climb aboard and feed on bits of dead skin. Studies done on cleaning stations suggest that the importance of this service varies from area to area. In one area where all the cleaners were removed, most of the other fish moved away, and those that didn't became infested with parasites. In other areas the results were less noticeable.

THE FISH

Many reef fish have small territories and you will see the same fish in the same place again and again.

Parrotfish

A coral-eating fish you will nearly always meet on the reef is the brightly colored parrotfish. There are several species and for the stoplight parrotfish (*Sparisoma viride*), rainbow parrotfish and midnight parrotfish, the names describe the colors. Not all are showy, but you can quickly recognize family members by their distinctive fused teeth which resemble a parrot's beak. Watch them use these teeth to scrape off chunks of coral (usually dead coral). The coral is passed to a remarkable mill in the back of the throat. There it is ground to a powder, the edible algae are digested, and the indigestible rocklike coral cement is excreted as sand. One study estimated that for every acre of reef, parrotfish produce about a ton of sand a year. Since they are daytime feeders, they are easy to watch, and if you follow one for a few minutes, you will see it contributing handsomely to some future beach.

Parrotfish, like many other fish, have complex sex lives. Regular males and females look much alike and from time to time a group will congregate and lay eggs together. However, should there be a shortage of males, some females will turn into males. They do this in a very dramatic manner. First they grow much bigger than other parrotfish; then they change color completely and grow the appropriate new sexual apparatus. These "terminal males" look quite unlike the ordinary males. They behave differently from ordinary males as well. Spurning the group scene, they select a particular female and spawn with her. Some studies show that after the sex change their senses are not all that they were, and they sometimes select males or juveniles to mate with by mistake. The ability of a species to change sex can be advantageous if the supply of normal males is seriously depleted by predators or storms. Many kinds of fish change sex.

While snorkeling you may see something that looks like a gelatinous plastic bag. This is likely to be the discarded night house of a parrotfish. Parrotfish create mucous bags which completely cover them before they go to sleep. This may hide them from predators. They do not always sleep in such a bag and no one knows exactly when and why they do.

Surgeonfish

Now and again you will come across a magnificent mixed species school of many fish, usually surgeonfish and parrotfish. Surgeonfish, such as the blue tang *(Acanthurus coeruleus)*, are recognizable by their shape. There are several species and they come in shades from pale blue through to dark blue and brown. Surgeonfish graze algae, often from dead coral. The name comes from a curious spine on either side of the body near the tail. This spine normally lies flat and is not noticeable, but if the fish feels threatened, the spine sticks straight out and it is as sharp as a surgeon's knife.

You might think that a large school of fish would be an easier target for a predator than a solitary individual. Studies show that this is not necessarily the case because predators get confused by the mass movement of all the fish.

Damselfish

One fish which is not very happy to see these big grazing schools is the little damselfish. All of the damselfish species are small and in their adult stage often a dull brown color. They tend to be fiercely territorial, defending their food, or their eggs, which they lay on the coral. You will often see one chasing away a fish much bigger than itself. So much bigger, in fact, that, should you encroach on its territory, it will come shooting out to attack you. It is quite instructive to do this just to watch them, and they are so small that they can hardly hurt you. One common Caribbean species, the three-spot damselfish, is a farmer. It chooses a patch of coral about one foot square, and scrapes away at its patch until the coral dies. Colonizing algae then grow over the dead coral. It then guards this crop against other fish, and feeds itself by taking occasional bites from its garden. If you observe one, you will see it eating, patrolling its territory, and chasing away other fish. If you follow a big school of grazing surgeonfish and parrotfish they may arrive at the farm of a three-spot damselfish. You then can watch the little fellow make a valiant effort to chase the marauders away, but while one is being repelled, another will sneak in and grab a snack from the farm.

Adult damselfish are usually drab, but some juveniles are striking. The yellowtail damselfish *(Microspathodon chrysurus)* starts out life exotically decked out in dark blue with glowing bright blue spots. They are eye catching and you will find them easy to remember.

Lizardfish
Synodus intermedius

The lizardfish, or sand diver fools its prey by using camouflage. It will turn a light color when on sand or darken to match another background. These are quite common and you will often see them in sand patches close to reefs. The lizardfish lies still in the sand, head sticking out and propped up on its fins. Like many bottom dwellers, it has no swim bladder and is a poor swimmer, but it is an excellent lunger and sits as still as a statue waiting for a fish to pass within striking distance.

Trumpetfish
Aulostomus maculatus

You will see the endearing, long, thin trumpetfish nearly every time you snorkel, but you may not recognize the fellow when you meet him a second time because trumpetfish, too, can change color. Yellow yesterday, blue today and tan tomorrow: the disguises are chosen to match the background. A tan trumpetfish often hangs, head down, waving with the currents among soft corals. From afar it looks innocent enough, but check out the actively moving eyes which reveal its predatory nature. A small fish that drifts too close will be sucked right in like a fly into a vacuum cleaner hose. This actor also keeps company with herbivores and can be seen accompanying a school of surgeonfish, dressed in matching blue. Again, he is up to no good and will slurp up small fish which trust the algae-eating surgeonfish. Even cleaning stations, those islands of trust in a carnivore-filled sea, are not sacred to the trumpetfish. Like a wolf in sheep's clothing, our friend will stay close to a fish who is going for a cleaning, and then suck the hygienist into its mouth.

Goatfish

A goatfish can be identified by the distinctive feelers on its chin which look like a pair of active white worms coming from the corners of its mouth. Goatfish swim along the bottom, stirring up the sand with these barbels in the hopes of finding a hiding invertebrate. They often forage together in small groups. The most commonly seen is the yellow goatfish (*Mulloidichthys martinicus*) which has a yellow stripe along its body, making it look a little like the yellowtail snapper. The snapper, however, lacks barbels. Watch for other kinds of fish following a goatfish, trying to capture some of the organisms that the feelers have stirred up.

Night feeding fish

There are several red-colored fish with big eyes. These fish are usually nocturnal, and the large eyes see well in dim light. While beautiful to look at, they are ordinairily at rest during the day, and so not very active. The most dramatic groupings you find are glassy sweepers (in the family Pempheridae) or squirrelfish (such as *Holocentrus rufus*). You may see hundreds of these packed together in a narrow crack in a wall, or in a tunnel or cave. They come out at night to feed. The squirrelfish is a bottom feeder and eats worms and small crustaceans on the sea bed. Bigeyes (*Priacanthus arenatus*) hang out singly, sheltering under coral ledges. They feed at night on small crustaceans that are found among the plankton. They used to be very common, but they are good to eat and have the unfortunate defence of turning themselves sideways to an enemy so they will look bigger. This has not proved very successful against spearfishing guns and their numbers have dwindled.

Not all night feeding fish are red. The French grunt (*Haemulon flavolineatum*) can also be seen by day hanging out in large schools. It has big eyes and yellow stripes. It ventures forth at night to feed on plankton.

Wrasse

If a fish is brightly colored and has a military bearing — with the body staying stiff and the pectoral fins doing all the work — it is probably a wrasse (in the family Labridae). There are some 500 species and it is one of the most well represented fish families on the reef. Wrasses feed by day, and many bury themselves at night under the sand. They are generally carnivorous and feed on invertebrates, including sea urchins. However, they are not completely carnivorous and if you take a little bread when you go snorkeling and let it disintegrate through your fingers, a bluehead wrasse (*Thalassoma bifasciatum*) is likely to be among the first to partake of the sudden bonanza. Like the parrotfish, the bluehead wrasse can change from female to male when the occasion demands. There are usually many more females than males and the males control the suitable spawning sites. The terminal males (males that began life as females) are easy to recognize because they have bright blue heads and characteristic body bands. Female blueheads come in several colors, but are most often yellow.

Porcupinefish One day you will be

peering into a crevice in the coral, or looking at a hole in a wreck, and you will come face to face with what looks like a huge fish with big eyes and a cherubic smile. This is most likely a porcupinefish (*Diodon hystrix*). These fish can grow to over two feet long, but even when they are smaller, they look big because their heads are large for their bodies. Porcupinefish have spines which normally lie flat, but when they get upset they puff themselves up into an oversized spiny ball. We once had the misfortune of anchoring a boat near some baby porcupinefish. One got curious about the water inlet which cooled the diesel-powered generator. The water suction trapped him and he puffed himself into a perfect plug, bringing the engine to a grinding halt. Porcupinefish teeth are fused together to make an efficient shell cracker and they feed on crabs, mollusks and other invertebrates. They have the unfortunate habit of getting caught on baited fishing hooks, and it takes thick gloves and considerable patience to retrieve the hook and leave the fish unharmed. (They are poisonous to eat.) They have cute faces and woeful eyes which make you wonder whether fishing is really worthwhile.

Vase sponge growing out of finger coral

Like most other reef fish, the porcupine fish is minute in its infancy and only vaguely resembles the adult. It drifts in the open sea as plankton which gives the offspring a chance, though a very slim one, of populating a new or distant reef. Adult fish cannot survive a long journey through the foodless sea, so the infants must do the exploring.

Trunkfish

There are several trunkfish (also known as boxfish) species. All members of the family are easily identified by their triangular shape. Seen from the front, the bottom of the fish is flat and the top is pointed. These fish sacrifice speed for bulk. They have a hard outer casing which both provides rigidity and turns off potential predators. Most of the time they move with slow dignity, like elderly aunts on an outing, but, if alarmed, they can show a surprising turn of speed. This, however, cannot be sustained for long. In addition to the hard casing, some trunkfish produce a poison from glands near the mouth that is harmful to potential predators. It even injures the trunkfish if it is in a confined space such as an aquarium.

A common boxfish species in the Caribbean is the smooth trunkfish (*Lactophrys triqueter*) which can be seen among coral and out over grassy areas. It eats small invertebrates, worms and crustaceans and sometimes finds its prey by blowing jets of water into the sand.

Angelfish

Angelfish are aristocratic looking and have beautiful faces. Angelfish and rock beauties (both in the family Pomacanthidae), are among the few fish able to stomach sponges which are both smelly and tough. The most colorful is the queen angelfish (*Holocanthus ciliaris*) with its rich blue, green and yellow coloring. It is easily distinguished by its "crown:" a circle of blue dots in a blue ring. The gray angelfish and French angelfish are also very handsome. The juveniles of both these species have curved light bands across their bodies.

Angel fish are generally unafraid of people and seeing these lovely fish just an arm's length away is one of the delights of snorkeling or diving.

SPONGES

Sponges are more beautiful and varied in the Caribbean than in any other of the world's seas. They come shaped like tubes, barrels and vases in colors that include bright yellow (yellow tube sponge, *Callyspongia plicifera*) and an amazing luminescent blue (azure vase sponge, *Aplysina fistularis*). These curious creatures are halfway between being a multi-celled animal and a colony of independent cells. Their cells can act very much as individuals, but also specialize to perform particular functions. In one experiment a sponge was put in a blender and then strained though a fine mesh cloth. After a day the sponge had put itself back together, much as it had been before. Many cells have hairlike whips (flagellae) which they beat back and forth to create a current. In a typical tube, barrel or vase sponge, water is drawn in through the outer surface of the sponge and pushed up through the central hollow. The current is too weak to be felt with your hand, but if you drop very fine particles from a foot or so above the sponge, they will be deflected by the current the sponge creates. The same cells that pump the water also have sticky collars. As the water flows through, food particles get stuck to these collars. Food is distributed by amoeba-like cells that float through the inside of the sponge like ghosts.

Sponges do not compete with corals for food as they feed on much smaller particles, some of which are smaller than bacteria. Many harbor vast populations of symbiotic bacteria and, paradoxically, are also a source of potent antibacterial compounds. Like soft corals, sponges can do well on lee shores and areas where plankton is scarce. They grow equally well on the reef, but here they compete with coral for a hard surface on which to anchor themselves. When coral gets damaged by grazing fish, sponges will often grow on the damaged area.

The tube and vaselike shapes make excellent hiding places. Look inside a few sponges and you are likely to find shrimps, small fish or brittle stars.

FOR MORE ABOUT CORAL REEFS

The creatures we have described are just a few of the many inhabitants of a Caribbean coral reef. "Divers and Snorkelers Guide to the Fishes and Sea Life of the Caribbean, Florida, the Bahamas and Bermuda," by F. Joseph Stokes, is an excellent identification book for reef fish. It includes some deep water fish as well. "A Field Guide to Coral Reefs of the Caribbean and Florida," the Peterson Guide by Eugene Kaplan, offers background information as well as helping with identification. Both books are small and easy to carry.

THE MANGROVE SWAMP

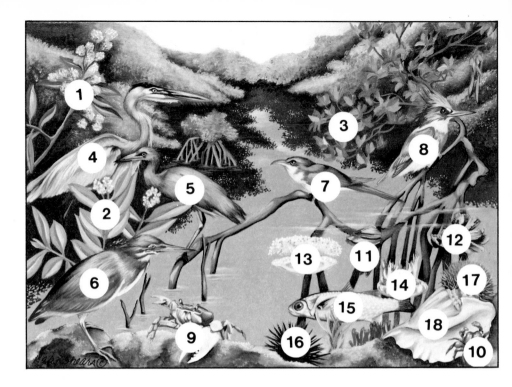

Plants

1. Button mangrove
2. Black mangrove
3. Red mangrove

Birds

4. Great blue heron
5. Little blue heron
6. Green-backed heron
7. Mangrove cuckoo
8. Belted kingfisher

Animals

9. Land crab
10. Mangrove tree crab

Underwater

11. Mangrove oyster
12. Flat tree oyster
13. Upsidedown jelly
14. Mangrove upsidedown jelly
15. White mullet
16. Long-spined black urchin
17. West Indian sea egg
18. Queen conch

In the topsy-turvy world of the mangroves, jellyfish lie on their backs, branching roots are high and dry in the air, and a lively crab dances in the tree tops, shunning the muddy tidal stream that sweeps in and out below.

"Mangrove" is not a precise term. It usually refers to woody plants from several plant families that can survive in the loose and muddy soils of tropical tide waters. Botanists don't agree on exactly what makes a mangrove, but mangrove swamps in the Caribbean are not hard to find. Look for red mangroves, trees that seem to walk into protected water on their strange arched prop roots. These roots trap and stabilize sediments so effectively that, in the course of a few hundred years, the red mangrove may be left high and dry on land of its own making. It has worked itself out of a job, because other mangrove species -- those that do less well on the water's edge, but better on mud -- will take over.

A mangrove swamp is one of the few habitats in the eastern Caribbean that can be buggy, particularly in the late afternoon. This feature, along with the fact that mangroves occupy a water's edge habitat that is coveted by developers, has in the past combined to give them an unwholesome reputation. Filling mangrove swamps and "reclaiming" the "wasted" real estate was once an acceptable activity. But the true value of mangroves is now more widely appreciated, and in a recent court decision a value of over $300,000 per acre was established for reconstituting a mangrove area damaged by an oil spill in Puerto Rico.

Birds come from all directions to roost and nest in mangroves. Cattle egrets and mangrove cuckoos come here after foraging on land. Frigatebirds and herons return to roost after patrolling the coastline, and pelicans settle here after their fishing expeditions.

The plant community is relatively simple, dominated by a few mangrove tree species and a fern, but it is a complex ecosystem to evaluate. The mangrove community receives nutrients from the land and transforms them into living material which is shipped out to sea with the tide. Coral reefs, seagrasses and mangroves are closely connected. The reefs serve as breakwaters that allow coastal mangroves to develop in quiet water. Seagrasses, too, slow currents and further calm the sea. The reef also provides sand which is added to the sediments in which both mangroves and seagrasses grow. This vegetation, in turn, provides energy for the reef ecosystem, for it is in the shelter of mangrove roots that countless young reef fish and small crustaceans find food and protection. Shrimp, too, begin here. Baby shrimp hide in the thick tangle of roots, grazing the thick black mud for bacteria and other tiny organisms which have multiplied on decomposing mangrove leaves. They remain in the dark recesses under the roots for one to three months with countless small conchs, crabs, worms and clams.

The economic benefits of a mangrove swamp are immense, but they are widely dispersed and indirect, unlike those of a field of bananas or a Caribbean pine plantation. Although mangroves benefit fisheries, provide timber, can stabilize a coastline, absorb the brunt of a hurricane's blow and filter out pollutants, they are bureaucratic orphans, which belong neither to fisheries or forestry or agriculture departments. The dispersed nature of their benefits means that a landowner can't cash in on them and they are not reflected in the market price of the land.

It is often said that mangroves extend the shoreline, but most of the sediments that they stabilize would be deposited even if no shoreline vegetation were present. It is more correct to say that they expedite the transition from gooey sediments to solid soils.

If you use insect repellent, you can explore this interesting habitat in peace. A small boat is your best approach. In many islands it is not hard to find a fisherman

Red mangroves

willing to use his boat as a taxi for the afternoon.

It is best to stay in the boat because penetrating the tangled roots and branches of a mangrove thicket on foot is a challenge. The slippery curved roots seem to be designed to throw you into the gooey mud and hands are more useful here than feet. Some scientists studying mangroves entertained themselves by having races: the world record for the 100-meter Mangrove Dash is believed to be 22 minutes and 30 seconds.

From afar the mangrove community looks monotonous. Most of the leaves are a bit fleshy, with smooth margins, and roughly the same size and shape. This may be because the different species are all adapted to survive in the same very difficult environment. The plants are anchored in loose soil, their roots are in oxygenless mud, their seeds fall into the sea and need to be seaworthy and, most important, they have to do something about salt.

Land plants and salt usually don't mix. Saline soils are a major problem in agriculture because most plants simply cannot tolerate salt. Salty water enters a plant's roots and, since plants lose water through evaporation and transpiration, the salt becomes concentrated until it poisons the plant. Mangroves have adaptations which enable them both to exclude some salt at their roots and to tolerate much more salt in their tissues than conventional plants. Black mangroves secrete salt through salt glands, which are scattered in individual shallow pits on the upper surface of the leaves. You can taste it on the leaves and it can even be collected for cooking or eating. If you wash or lick the salt off and then wait a few minutes, you will find that a new layer of salt has been excreted. Red mangroves do not secrete salt; instead they keep most of it from entering their roots. Red mangrove sap has only one tenth the salt concentration of the black mangrove. However, even mangroves can't tolerate extreme levels of salt. Without rain, the concentration of salt, and sometimes of sulfides, builds to a lethal level in the soil. Some mangroves depend on a flush of fresh water at least once a year. Hurricanes limit the height of mangroves by knocking them

Green-backed heron

back periodically, but they also may bring a needed deluge of fresh water. If freshwater streams are diverted or used for agriculture, the mangroves may suffer.

Salinity makes it more difficult for plants to take up water. Every drop they take up is full of salt. You may notice that the adaptations of mangroves are similar to those of plants of dry areas: a thick waxy coating on the leaves and succulent leaves for storing water.

Most mangroves grow very well in fresh water, but they are ordinarily excluded from these environments by other plants which don't have the expense of maintaining complex desalination equipment. Salt water plays an important role in the mangrove plant community: it keeps potential competitors out.

PLANTS

Red mangrove
Rhizophora mangle

This is a tree that has seedlings but no seeds - the phase of a plant that involves sitting around doing nothing. Like several other mangrove species, the seedling begins to grow while still attached to the parent tree. It grows into a long thin cigar, and you can see many of these hanging from the branches. They are the new plants' roots, a big head start for the seedlings which are about to set off on a hazardous sea journey. A seedling can stay alive while afloat for up to a year and leaves and side roots may shoot out while the seedling is drifting. Before long, the root end absorbs water and tips downwards. If carried to a shallow spot, it may root. If the spot is calm, it will stay rooted and can grow up to three feet in its first year. The unmistakable arched prop roots begin by the third year. These are roots and not stems, and this kind of support system is common among plants growing on silty waterlogged soil.

The red mangrove supports itself not only with prop roots that come out of the stems but also with drop roots which dangle from branches high on the tree. Red mangroves can be identified by their long-pointed terminal buds as well as by their roots.

The above-ground part of the prop and drop roots is well supplied with small pores (lenticels) that allow oxygen to diffuse into the root and travel though air-filled chambers to the below-ground part of the root. At high tide the greasy lenticels keep water out. These two root types, plus the normal roots, all end in a fine network of feeding roots, just like those of other plants.

Usually red mangroves grow farther seaward than the other mangrove species and they are at home in the saltiest sea water. Red mangroves are native to the tropical and subtropical coasts of America, West Africa and some Pacific islands.

One reason the ecological importance of mangroves was underestimated in the past is that when old leaves die and drop into the water, they just lie there, uneaten. This made people think they were wasted. Only recently have scientists looked more closely at the fate of mangrove detritus. To begin with, there is a lot of it: at more than three tons per acre per year, the productivity of a red mangrove swamp is higher than that of most terrestrial ecosystems.

When a red mangrove leaf falls into the water, it contains about 3% protein. It is almost immediately colonized by microorganisms which convert compounds such as cellulose and lignin into digestible proteins. Many bacteria and fungi prefer to dine on cellulose and they leave the protein. By the time a leaf is fully colonized, the protein concentration has risen from 3% to 22%. The nutritious microorganisms are eaten by invertebrates and fish. Leaf particles may be eaten and excreted over and over again, with each consuming animal assimilating different compounds. Fallen mangrove leaves and twigs are, in fact, the beginning of a complex food web that includes many commercially important species of shrimp, crabs and fish.

Black mangrove
Avicennia germinans

You usually find black mangroves on the shore side of a swampy area, often just inland of red mangroves, but they may be the pioneers where greater wave or tidal action excludes the red mangroves. They range farther to the north and south than the other mangroves, but cannot tolerate frost. They also can survive greater fluctuations in salinity and put up with soil that contains almost no oxygen.

The lower surface of the leaves is hairy and silvery and the small fruits are pale green, flattened and pear shaped. The seeds often germinate on the tree and the fallen seedlings float, just like those of the red mangrove.

Hoards of strange looking knobby wooden sticks poke out of the mud from the horizontal roots of black mangroves. These are pneumatophores, a plant's version of an air shaft. They are specialized structures that grow upwards from the roots and supply the roots with air. Roots need oxygen, and in the mud around mangrove roots, decomposing organisms have used it all. Gaseous oxygen must be pumped from above the water surface, just as it is done in the Holland Tunnel. The red mangrove's prop roots perform the same function.

Black mangroves get rid of salt by excreting it onto the leaf surface, but they also exclude salt at the roots. The concentration of salt in the sap is high, but still only about one tenth that of seawater.

Mangroves are extremely susceptible to pollution. Their battle with salt puts them under constant metabolic stress. In addition, their breathing system of lenticels and pneumatophores is vulnerable to being clogged by anything oily. A mangrove swamp in Vietnam did not recover from a single dose of pesticide that was applied 14 years earlier.

White mangrove
Laguncularia racemosa

White mangroves typically grow on the mud that black and red mangroves have consolidated. They are less tolerant of endless soaking in salt water, but can be the pioneers on sandy spits.

The leaf stalks, or petioles, have two conspicuous raised gland dots just below the base of the leaf. The opposite leaves are long ovals, pointed at both ends. You can usually see grains of salt on the leaves, for this is another salt-secreting species. The small fruits are velvety gray-green and look like little flattened ribbed bags, bunched together at the tops.

Occasionally the seeds germinate on the tree, but more often they fall and float for about four weeks. Then they sink and begin growing when submerged. Lucky seeds sink in shallow water.

Buttonwood
Conocarpus erectus

Some say that buttonwood is not a true mangrove, but a "mangrove associate" because its tolerance for salt is limited and it lacks the peculiarly mangrove features such as pneumatophores, prop roots, or having its seeds germinate on the tree.

Buttonwood is the only Caribbean mangrove (if it is a mangrove) with alternate leaves. Otherwise, it looks much like the other mangroves, except that its leaves are even more sharply pointed. It has minute greenish flowers which are crowded into balls (the "buttons"). These eventually turn brown. This species grows where the soil is only moderately salty and where tides only occasionally flood the surface. It is the only common mangrove that is naturally resistant to marine borers.

The wood of all four mangrove species has many uses. Poles and posts are made from mangroves and buttonwood wood takes a high polish and has been used in turning and boatbuilding. Black mangrove is rarely sawn, but is used for masts and telephone poles. Mangrove wood burns slowly and is excellent for fuel. It also makes high quality charcoal.

The bark of mangroves is rich in tannins and these have been used extensively. Often the water nearby will be stained brown from tannins which have leached from the roots and stems. Herbal medicines and a dye are made from the bark. Bees that feed from the flowers of white and black mangrove are reputed to produce very good honey.

Other names: button mangrove, gray mangrove.

Mangrove fern
Acrostichium aureum

Mangrove ferns are found among mangroves and in other coastal habitats around the world. The fronds are dark green above and rusty below because the undersides of the leaves are covered with brown spore cases. This large tough fern gets by in situations that would instantly kill most of its tender relatives. The frond is plain, not at all lacy and the epidermis is thick. This both limits water loss and acts somewhat as a sunblock, for mangrove ferns are often exposed to the intense tropical sun. Near the base of the leaf stalk there is often a long light colored strip of tissue. This is a pneumatophore, acting to bring air to the roots, just as the pencil-like projections do for the black mangrove. Unlike some mangrove trees, the mangrove fern does not have a way to get rid of salt. The tissues are so laden with salt that they are quite fire resistant. Central American Indians figured this out and used the fronds to thatch areas of their huts that are nearest the hearth.

Swamp bloodwood, bois mang
Pterocarpus officinalis

You sometimes find swamp bloodwood trees up rivers, on the inshore side of mangroves. The leaves of this very large tree are usually too high to see, but it is easily identified by its strange buttress roots. These enormous structures are often several feet high and ten or more feet long. They meander sinuously across the ground. The light brown inner bark is streaked with a blood red color. One of the best places to see these trees in the Eastern Caribbean is on the Indian River in Dominica.

There has been a lot of discussion about whether buttresses are tension or compression members. A recent detailed investigation suggests that there is no clear answer to that question. They are common where soils are wet or loose and they may simply provide a broad platform that minimizes toppling.

BIRDS

Mangrove cuckoo
Coccyzus minor

In the dense, dark green shade of mangroves, the mangrove cuckoo is more likely to be heard than seen. You may hear a scratchy guttural qua-qua-qua as this shy bird flies through the trees like a shadow. These cuckoos also spend time in dry areas or secondary forests where it is easier to see them. They are medium sized birds, about 12 to 13 inches long, are brown above, have buffy underparts and wear a handsome black mask. The underside of the long tail is boldly banded with black and white. Mangrove cuckoos eat mostly insects, but will take some fruits and berries. Unlike Old World cuckoos, these birds build their own nests and raise their own young. A frail, flat nest of twigs is built in a dense thicket.

Swamp bloodwood

Belted kingfisher
Ceryle alcyon

Kingfishers are chunky birds with blue gray heads, backs and chest bands. Both sexes have white collars, but the female outshines her handsome mate by also having a band of chestnut across her belly. The large crested heads of kingfishers make them look top-heavy. An obvious white wing patch will help you identify these birds when they are flying. They make an hysterical-sounding rattle when upset. They perch over water on wires or dead branches and catch fish by plunge-diving into the water. Kingfishers breed in North America and, like many other North Americans, are most likely to be seen in the Caribbean from October to April.

Other names: martin-pecheur, kingfisher-man.

Green-backed heron, small green heron
Butorides striatus

These small members of the true heron family average about 18 inches in length, compared to the great blue heron's 45 inches. They fly with their dumpy legs, noticeably short for a heron, dangling. The tail, too, is short. The back is a steely gray green, with a gloss of purple, and the head and throat are chestnut. Green-backed herons make a terrible squalling snarl when disturbed. None of their several noises is even remotely musical.

The nest is a messy platform of sticks in dense vegetation over water. Three to four greenish eggs are laid and the adventurous young herons soon learn to climb around in the nesting tree, using their feet, wings and bill, long before they can fly.

Green-backed herons slowly stalk their prey of fish, crabs and shrimp in shallow water or maneuver across mangrove prop roots, eyes fixed to the water, waiting for something to come within striking distance. Lizards and grasshoppers, found near water, supplement the fishy diet.

Little blue heron, small gray gaulin
Egretta caerulea

You may see a graceful slate-gray heron keeping close company with a snow white heron of the same shape and size. Alas, this does not herald the arrival of the peaceable kingdom. It is, instead, a mother little blue heron with her offspring. The first full set of feathers that the young birds grow is almost pure white. They molt to slate gray when a year old. The head and neck of the adult are a dull maroon color.

The little blue heron fishes with a stately elegance, delicately making its way along the shore. A startlingly fast jab at a fish disrupts the peaceful scene. Lizards, crabs and insects are also eaten. Like most other herons, little blues fly with their necks doubled back, the head resting on the shoulders and the long legs trailing behind the short tail.

Up on top of the mangroves you may see the little blue herons' nests. These are frail platforms of sticks, loosely held together, and they have no lining. The female usually lays three to four pale bluish green eggs and both parents incubate them.

Great blue heron, large gray gaulin
Ardea herodias

At 42 to 52 inches long, and with a wingspan of seven feet, the great blue heron is almost twice as big as either the little blue or the green-backed heron. Another common visitor from North America, this is a large slate-colored bird with considerable white on its head and neck. When alarmed it will give out a long harsh croak. This heron seems to prefer fresh or brackish water to salt and it may be found well inland if there is a freshwater pond or lake. In flight its huge wings flap slowly and majestically and its long legs stretch out behind. The great blue heron uses the sit-and-wait fishing strategy, often standing motionless for a long time before a fish ventures within its reach. Great blues also eat crabs, lizards, crayfish, grasshoppers and mice.

Mangrove tree crab
Aratus pisonii

Mangrove tree crabs are small, less than an inch across the carapace, but there are so many of them that you will certainly see one. We find sitting in a boat close to the mangroves and scanning red mangrove branches with binoculars to be quite effective. They are a dark olive brown, tinged with reddish brown and their beady eyes are far apart, at the outside corners of the carapace. Trying to get closer than about eight feet from a tree crab is probably a futile exercise. Crabs of several species will climb trees occasionally, but only mangrove tree crabs have sharp tips on the ends of their legs, are very agile and almost completely arboreal. They live, feed and mate in mangrove trees, dropping into the water only to avoid predators. They supplement their mangrove leaf diet with insects, and will sometimes eat dead fish.

Mangrove tree crabs must return to the sea at breeding time. This is quite usual for land crabs for they originated in the sea, and few have managed to evolve a terrestial breeding habit. The juvenile stages still develop in their ancestral medium. Females walk down a prop root to the water's edge when it is time to shed their hatching eggs. There they fan their abdomens to wash off all the eggs. One scientist has estimated that 99.97% of the hatchlings will perish during their month in the currents, before they develop into the adult, tree-dwelling form. When the few survivors climb up the roots to begin their lives as leaf eaters, they tend to stay near the water, perhaps to avoid the bigger, canopy-dwelling adults which might find the little morsels irresistible.

Land crab, white crab
Cardisoma guanhumi

The flat area back from the water's edge, which the red mangrove turned from sea to dry land, is only a foot or two above sea level and often is dotted with large holes. These are the entrances to the long curved burrows of the white crab, often called the land crab. This crab is the most commonly eaten crab in the Caribbean. The burrows go down to the water table, for the white crab needs almost constant access to water and can come out only at night or when it is raining. The ground surrounding the burrows is often so clean that it looks as though it has been swept, for white crabs are mainly herbivores and eat just about anything within about eight inches of the ground. They can be very large, to almost four inches across the shell, are gray, blue-gray or light yellow and pop into their burrows when approached.

The reason they are "mainly" herbivores is that they don't have access to much else, as they are too slow to be effective predators. They will eat carrion when it is available and they also cannibalize young crabs, though in the lab scientists have found that the amount of cannibalism is related to the crabs' diet. If given vegetable food that is rich in nitrogen, cannibalism is uncommon. But when nitrogen is scarce, it's crab eat crab. Nitrogen, in a form they can use, may be a limiting resource for these animals, as their usual food contains only 0.5 to 2% nitrogen by dry weight, compared with the 7 to 14% nitrogen found in meat. In addition, these crabs have small gut volumes and long gut cycling times - up to 24 hours - which further limits the amount of nitrogen they can assimilate.

Though cannibalism of young crabs may at first seem counterproductive, it may be an effective feedback loop for population regulation. A cannibalistic white crab is very unlikely to consume its own offspring because crab reproduction involves several developmental stages in the sea, after which the offspring come ashore at random, usually far from mom and dad. The presence of a stint at sea, where the newly hatched larvae feed and undergo several molts over a period of about a month, also means that when the little ones come ashore, they are walking CARE packages, containing scarce nutrients from an environment which is unavailable to the adult white crabs.

Both males and females have one claw that is larger than the other, though the size difference is greater in males. The large claw is used for signaling and combat, mostly over females, as opposed to food. Mating takes place during the rainy season, outside of the burrows, one or two days before a new or a full moon. About a month later there is a mass migration to the sea's edge, where the hatching of the fully developed eggs takes place. Soon after hatching they are shaken into the water.

Land crabs are a delicacy in most islands. The crabs are cooked, then the meat is removed, spiced and returned to the carapace (shell) for a dish called "crab back." Some people purge crabs by feeding them a diet of cornmeal and coconut in case they have eaten manchineel leaves.

In some situations white crabs are quite unpopular because they make what one writer has called 18,000-hole golf courses, each hole with a large heap of soil around the entrance. This is a landscaping technique not currently in vogue for front lawns.

Buttonwood

UNDERWATER

Mangrove oyster
Crassostrea species
Flat tree oyster
Isognomon alatus

Both of these oysters are small and full of mud when they are picked from the prop roots of the red mangrove. When carefully prepared, they are both delicious and are much sought after for food. People are not the only problem for these oysters. Starfish can pry the shells apart and so can some sharp-billed birds.

Mangrove oysters have long purple shells and are most often found in brackish water. The flat tree oyster has a gray shell and is more common in more saline environments. The interior of the shell is stained with brown, purple or black. Both

54

Land crab

grow in clusters and will colonize pilings, shipwrecks and rocks as well as mangroves.

Upsidedown jelly
Cassiopeia frondosa
Mangrove upsidedown jelly
Cassiopeia xamachana

If you peer into the shallow water near mangroves, you may see a gently pulsating jellyfish flat on its back looking as though it is having a problem. But upsidedown is right side up for both these related jellyfish. When in this position more sunlight gets to the single-celled yellow-brown algae (zooxanthellae) that live among their tentacles and provide much of the jellyfish's food. Jellyfish are related to corals which have a similar symbiotic relationship with algae. Both groups also use stinging cells, called nematocysts, for capturing prey and for defense. The *Cassiopeias* are harmless to mildly toxic. They may cause red welts if you touch them. When swimming, these jellyfish look normal, but they flop over on their backs when they are just hanging out.

"Cassiopeia" was a mythical queen who was turned into a constellation by a group of gods who favored her. She was then positioned in the sky by another group of gods who were her bitter rivals. These gods placed her so far north that she appears upsidedown for much of the year, a punishment for her vanity.

The upsidedown jelly is yellowish brown and commonly grows to five inches across. Its dome is rather flat and the tentacles fan out to the same radius as the dome. The edges of the dome of the mangrove upsidedown jelly, which usually grows to about seven inches, are curled inwards and the tentacles curve in as well, wrapped around their own lacy edges.

West Indian sea egg
Tripneustes ventricosus

Among the seagrasses you may see the West Indian sea egg, an urchin with half-inch white spines, which grows to about five inches in diameter. Sea urchins have radially symmetric bodies which are covered with protective spines. The flattened spherical shell is called a test and in this species is a dark color: brown, purple or black. The opening at the bottom is the mouth. It is surrounded by five teeth used for scraping up algae and for eating turtle grass. The anus is at the top.

The eggs (roe) of the West Indian sea egg are eaten and the animals are scarce in some areas. Roe can be eaten raw, usually with a splash of lime juice. Sometimes the roe from several urchins is put into one urchin shell, which is then roasted over a fire.

These urchins are found on shallow reefs during the day. Often they pick up blades of seagrass or debris and stick these on their spines as camouflage.

Like other urchins, they are important because they eat algae on coral reefs, preventing the algae from smothering the coral. Hurricanes sometimes kill off large numbers of sea eggs. There has been a ban on taking sea eggs in St. Lucia since 1987 to allow the population to recover.

Other names: white sea urchin, chadon.

Long-spined black urchin
Diadema antillarum

The long-spined black urchin is common and hazardous. If you put your hand near one (not too near), it will move its menacing spines, up to a foot long, to point at you. The sharp spines can penetrate clothing, wet suits, sneakers and even flippers and they carry an irritating toxin into the wound. They are hollow and so brittle that they break off, leaving you with a glassy spike in your foot. But fortunately the sting, like that from a bee, does not last more than a few hours. The calcareous spines are almost impossible to remove, but luckily they are absorbed in a few days. This process can be speeded by bathing the area in a weak acid, such as lime juice.

Like many other creatures that sting, bite and poke us when we step on them, the long-spined black urchin is not all bad and it, too, has a role to play in the coastal ecosystem. In 1983 and 1984 these urchins mysteriously died off in great numbers throughout the Caribbean and the algae that they normally feed on were growing unchecked. It was feared that these algae would overgrow and smother corals, but, just as mysteriously, the urchin populations began to recover. Urchins also provide areas for coral larvae to settle by grazing the algae from rocks and dead coral patches. You can often see newly

hatched shrimps taking refuge among the urchin's sharp spines. Long-spined urchins feed at night on detritus and turtle grass as well as on algae.

The sedentary looking black urchin can walk by using short spines at the base of the shell, somewhat as we would use crutches. They can just barely outrun their enemy the sea star, but they can chemically sense the presence of a sea star and get a head start. The queen triggerfish is another enemy. It turns the urchins over and attacks the unprotected center.

Queen conch, lambi
Strombus gigas

Conchs are snails, a class which contains over 35,000 species and is in the group called mollusks. In Latin "mollusca" means "soft bodied" and, indeed, these animals do not have a true skeleton. Instead most mollusks secrete a shell from a layer of specialized tissue called a mantle.

The queen conch can grow to 12 inches. At this size the shell weighs about a pound and a half and the animal weighs a half pound.

"Operculum" is the name given to a snail's front door, the toenail-like disk that protects the animal when it has withdrawn into its shell. In the conch this structure is modified into a claw-like tool. The conch uses this as a pole vault. By anchoring it the sand it can awkwardly leap forward.

You are unlikely to see a fully grown conch because they are delicious to eat and have been over-harvested in most places. But, though they now are scarce in shallow water, they have the capacity to recover. After fertilization, the female deposits an egg cluster of half a million eggs in a sandy area near grass beds. The tiny hatchlings, called veligers, swim up to the surface of the sea and travel for a month in the current before settling to the bottom. Until they are fairly large, they are easy prey for turtles, crabs, lobsters, octopuses and many fish. They bury themselves in the sand by day, coming out only at night to feed on seagrasses. They are nearly full size at three or four years. The lip of the shell

56

flares and becomes thickened and after this they do not grow appreciably.

White mullet
Mugil curema

If you see a large light-colored fish jump clear of the water and land with a loud splat, it is likely to be the white mullet. But, just why it indulges in this behavior is not known. It may be blasting parasites off its body. Mullets are among the few fish this big that use the bottom of the food chain directly. They strain tiny organisms from the mud. Most fish of this size are higher on the food chain, eating shrimp and crabs that have gotten fat doing the dirty work.

Manatee grass
Syringodium filiforme
Turtle grass
Thalassia testudinum

Manatee grass and turtle grass have something in common with dolphins and whales: both the grasses and the mammals have evolved from terrestrial forms. These grasses have true, though tiny, flowers and their pollen and seeds flow in the currents just as more ordinary pollen and seeds ride the wind. They reproduce mainly by spreading roots but, unlike the seaweeds, they also can make real seeds. Seagrasses are the only flowering plants that spend their entire lives submerged in seawater.

Turtle grass and manatee grass are the most common species, but there are other seagrasses. Turtle grass is the broad-bladed one (like medium noodles). Manatee grass is fine and the blades are round (like vermicelli).

Large beds of these green-brown grasses grow in shallow water. Here they baffle and slow the ocean currents, and this increases the sedimentation of both organic and inorganic matter. Their dense tangled roots hold these deposits. These grass beds are highly productive, but since most animals do not find the grass blades palatable or digestible, more blades enter the food chain as detritus than as fresh greens.

The leaves do present a big surface area for algae which grow as epiphytes and in one area 113 species of algae were found on the turtle grass. Conchs may only assimilate the epiphytes. As with mangrove leaves, the chewed-up grass itself is excreted and colonized by another group of feeders, and so on. Some invertebrates simply use turtle grass for shelter.

Other animals make good use of turtle grass, too. The long-spined black sea urchin hides in crevices in the reef by day, and feeds on turtle grass at night. You will notice that grasses rarely grow right up to the edge of a reef because the urchins feed most heavily here, close to the safety of the reef. Parrotfish and surgeonfish, too, feed directly on turtle grass. These fish do not dare forage far from the protection of the reef for fear of barracuda which often station themselves above the grass looking out for careless grazers. The green turtle (*Chelonia mydas*) also eats turtle grass. An analysis of 202 green turtle stomach contents showed that 87% of the turtles' diet was turtle grass.

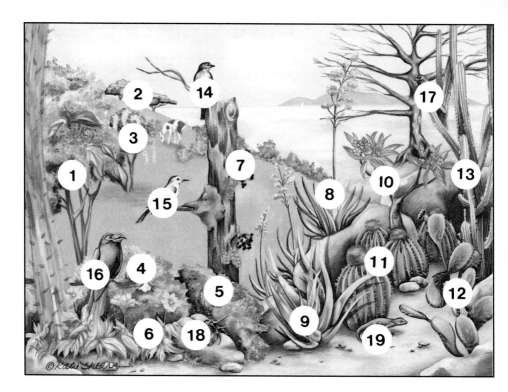

Plants

1. Fiddlewood
2. Acacia
3. Logwood
4. Sea island cotton
5. Kannik
6. West Indian marigold
7. Crab's eyes
8. Century plant
9. Aloe
10. Frangipani
11. Turk's head cactus
12. Prickly pear cactus
13. Organ pipe cactus

Birds

14. Caribbean elaenia
15. Mockingbird
16. Ani
17. Black-faced grassquit

Animals

18. Hermit crab
19. Ground lizard

In late summer and fall the low sparsely-vegetated coastal land gets soaked with rain and you may wonder why on earth this is called dry scrub. But come in late winter to early spring, when rainless sunny days and strong winds have parched the soil, and you will see that many plants have died back to below ground level or shed their leaves, shutting down to preserve enough moisture to maintain a flicker of life.

This is the driest terrain in the islands. Trees right on the beach generally stay green, for here any rain that falls floats on the saltwater below and is accessible to plants. Back from the beach, rainwater sinks deep into the soil, beyond the reach of plants. Century plants and cactuses stay green, as do a few leathery-leaved rough shrubs. Some of the shrubs look as though they would be happier if they, too, could shed their pathetically wilting leaves.

The plants and animals here must all adapt to seasonal drought if they are to survive. Grazing animals, such as sheep and goats, are a major threat to dry scrub plants. A lot of water is needed to replace a nibbled leaf or twig, and nearly all the plants bristle with defensive thorns

Some plants, instead of shedding their foliage, have fleshy succulent leaves which are used to store water to help carry them through a dry period. Leathery leaves with thick waxy cuticles also help reduce water loss through evaporation.

Acacias and other trees are widely spaced. It looks as though there is room for many more on the broad open fields, but, under the surface and out of sight, the roots of these trees meet each other. They extend far beyond the leafy crowns in their urgent search for water. In a study of a dry forest in Puerto Rico, it was found that 50% of the living plant matter was below ground; a much higher proportion than for any other known forest. Acacia roots are fighting for precious water underground, just as more normal trees struggle against each other for a place in the sun.

In pre-human times deciduous forest covered much of the land that is now in shrubby acacia, croton and cactus. Years of farming these thin soils have left them too depleted to support a forest again. Added to this is the 100-year old tradition of releasing goats and cows in December or January, after corn and peas are harvested. The animals are caught back again in May or June when planting occurs, but by then perennial crops like trees have been destroyed.

With the first heavy rain in May or June, the gray-brown scrub vegetation miraculously turns green overnight. But if rain falls in January, near the beginning of the dry season, the vegetation will not awaken.

PLANTS

Century plant

Agave caribaeicola

Century plants grow in a stemless rosette of fleshy, swordlike, prickly leaves, each ending with a vicious thorn. The plants grow for years, slowly becoming larger and storing enough food for the crowning event of their lives. After 10 to 20 years (rarely a century), a gigantic flower stalk emerges. It grows very rapidly, to a height of twenty feet or more. One plant in Grenada was measured every day for nine days and during this time grew an astounding eight feet and nine inches. The brilliant yellow flowers usually come out in April. After the flowers fade, the whole plant dies. Sometimes small offshoots of the parent plant will take over. Little bulblets form among the flowers and these, too, are capable of beginning a new plant. There also are seeds.

Many people are familiar with plants that use red flowers to attract pollinating hummingbirds, but a similar relationship between bats and flowers is less well known. Bats, like hummingbirds, are important pollinators. They are strong flyers, able and willing to carry pollen for long distances.

Century plant flowers may be full of hummingbirds and insects by day, but they are designed to attract bats. Bats need more protein than insects do and the pollen of bat-pollinated plants typically has twice as much protein as does the pollen of related plants that are pollinated by insects. In addition to upping the protein content, century plants tailor their flowers to bats in other ways. The flowers open at night and release butyric acid, a batty smelling substance. Butyric acid attracts bat to bat as well as bat to flower. The flowers are arranged on bat serving trays, high above the leaves and at night the yellow flowers stand out like fluorescent bat beacons.

Bats are a good choice for century plants, a Caribbean native. Most mammals have a difficult time colonizing small islands, but bats have no trouble, and there are both many bat species and many bats.

Century plants led to the discovery of a very different metabolic pathway from the one used by most plants. This procedure is known as Crassulacean acid metabolism, or CAM. Plants cannot normally store carbon dioxide. They take in carbon dioxide during the day through pores (stomates), and use it in the process of photosynthesis. This is accompanied by a lot of water loss through the open stomates. Plants using CAM open their stomates to take in carbon dioxide at night, when it is cooler and the humidity is higher. All night long they store carbon dioxide by converting it into organic compounds, usually malic acid. When the sun comes out in the morning, the water-losing stomates close and photosynthesis takes place using the carbon dioxide in the malic acid. It is a less efficient form of photosynthesis, but saves a lot of water. Agaves are able to keep their leaves, even when it is very dry, perhaps in part because of this water-saving system.

CAM has since been found to occur in the dry-dwelling members of 30 other plant families, including cactuses.

Agaves are used pharmacologically in the synthesis of such things as cortisone and estrogen. The sap from the leaf has long been used by herbalists for skin complaints and other parts are used for food, shampoo, soap, rope and medicines.

Other names: agave, lang bef.

Aloe
Aloe barbadensis

Everyone should get to know the aloe, because the gooey substance that oozes from the broken leaves can be wiped directly on the skin and makes a first-rate treatment for burns, including sunburn. Aloe originated in the Mediterranean countries. This may lead you to wonder why the species name is *barbadensis*, suspiciously like Barbados. It was so named because this aloe was extensively cultivated in Barbados in colonial times. The medicinal usefulness of aloe was first recorded in 400 B.C. and it has been grown and spread by humans ever since.

This aloe now grows wild throughout the West Indies and is perfectly at home on thin dry soils. The spiny, grayish-green leaves are very fleshy and are often tinged with red. There is no stem until the flower comes along. The flower stalk arises from the center of the leaves, grows to 30 inches high, and supports many one inch yellow flowers.

The plant has the same format as the agave, but is easily distinguished. Agaves are stringy: rope is made from the fibers in their leaves, whereas aloe leaves are readily broken and have no reinforcing. They are more like bags of imperfectly-set gelatin. Aloes flower annually and agaves take many years to flower.

Aloe flowers are reported to be a good-tasting addition to a fruit salad, but aloe is far better appreciated for its medicinal, rather than its culinary, attributes. It seems to have been used herbally for most of the

A century plant in flower. The tree to the right of the century plant is an acacia.

ills the flesh is heir to: the goo from broken leaves is used to help wounds heal, as a tea for colds, for headaches, diabetes and in some islands has been used on children's fingers to discourage them from sucking their fingers. It is used for sore throats and as a shampoo or hair conditioner. The slimy center of a leaf, beaten with an egg white and some honey, has been taken for upset stomach. For earache and eye troubles, a mixture of aloe and sterile water has been applied.

Gumbo limbo
Bursera simaruba

How does a tree come to have more than 50 common names? Is it because the tree, in this case gumbo limbo, is so eye-catching and appealing that everyone who looks at it wants to capture its essence in a name? Its glowing red-orange bark and the graceful fluid pattern of its branches draw the attention of blase sunbathers and utilitarian locals alike.

Gumbo limbo is a medium-sized tree of both the very dry and the moist forests in the Caribbean region. It is sometimes seen quite near the beach and can withstand some salt spray. It is most common on dry, rocky, limestone hills, but the trees grow bigger in rich valleys. Tiny flowers grow in clusters at the ends of the branches and the male and female flowers occur on separate trees. The fruits reach full size a week after the flowers are pollinated, but they ripen on the tree for the next eight months, slowly turning from green to purple.

Gumbo limbo has many adaptations to drought. It is deciduous, and loses its leaves before all the other trees. Yellowish gumbo limbos signal the beginning of the dry season. Beneath the thin reddish bark, a green bark layer photosynthesizes throughout the dry season. The wood is very soft, so soft that it can be cut with a cutlass, and the entire stem swells when rain is plentiful. The stored water helps during a dry patch. Gumbo limbos can survive most hurricanes. The leaves and small twigs are blown off, but the tree quickly recovers.

Some think that its bark peels to prevent epiphytes from getting a firm grip. It may also be that the slippery bark prevents rats from climbing the tree and that this is why gumbo limbos are frequently chosen by birds for roosting and nesting.

The wood is used for lumber and fuel, primarily because of its abundance, rather than because of its superior qualities. The leaves are fed to sheep and goats. A pitchy-smelling resin which oozes from cuts in the bark is used locally as a cheap glue, as varnish, for coating canoes and for incense. The caribs used the latex of this tree as a poultice for bruises or plastered it to strained areas of the body for relief. The leaves have been used as a substitute for tea.

Other names: turpentine tree, West Indian birch, birch, naked Indian, gommier rouge, gommier maduit, gommier barriere, tourist tree, etc.

Acacia
Acacia nilotica

Acacias are among the most common trees in dry scrubby areas. They are small, branchy trees, usually wider than high. Often the foliage has a grayish cast. Worldwide, there are some 600 species of acacia and almost all have yellow flowers in balls. In this species the flower balls are just over a half inch in diameter. There are many kinds in the Caribbean; usually called cassie by the locals. Most of them are armed with long, sharp spines. The young trees are even more densely spiny than older ones. The spines grow in pairs at the base of the leaves and in this species are from one half to one and a half inches long. They exist solely to deter the grazing animals that menace all plants of dry open spaces. Acacias shed most or all of their leaves during the dry season.

Acacia nilotica is widespread in Africa and was imported for the gum it produces.

The seedpods of this species are grayish, flattened and pinch in between the seeds. The tiny leaflets are arranged on three to eight pairs of side axes of the leaf.

Crab's eyes
Abrus precatorius

The slender stems of this twining woody vine form tangles as they scramble up bushes and small trees. When the black seed pods mature and dry, they twist open, revealing flaming red and black seeds. The seeds are very small, but they are so bright that they will lead you to notice the rest of the plant which may grow to be fifteen feet long.

Crab's eyes is native to tropical Asia, but now is found world-wide in the tropics. The glossy seeds are so poisonous that one thoroughly chewed seed can kill a child. They are often strung for necklaces, but are softened by boiling before they are strung, and boiling destroys the poison. The seeds are sometimes dangerous to livestock, but insects seem to know that the seeds spell trouble: they are never nibbled. The seeds were formerly used in India and Africa for weighing gold.

Most of the other parts of the plant have been experimented with. The roots and stems have been used as a substitute for licorice. The leaves have been used with other plants to make a syrup to treat chronic asthma. The plant has been used to stop hemorrhaging in women.

Other names: jumbie beads, wire wiss, liquorice plant, lickrish, gwen l' gliz (literally, seeds of the church)

Turk's cap cactus
Melocactus intortus

Cactuses are green throughout the dry season. It is the branches that are green, a part of their single-minded campaign to save water. Cactuses are the camels of the plant world. They have shallow, spreading root systems to collect every drop of water that falls. When there is extra, it is stored in the fluted stems which can expand to make plenty of room. Fluting also gives the stem more surface area for photosynthesizing. Like century plants, cactuses use the CAM method to photosynthesize. Fierce spines, which are technically modified leaves sprout in bunches, pointing every which way to deter foragers. The spines help small birds which can safely nest among them. Birds eat the cactus fruits and disperse the seeds.

Turk's cap cactuses are nearly round and sit, like prickly balls, right on the ground. They tend to tilt towards the equator, which has earned them the name compass plants. The fuchsia-colored fruits are eaten by people, as well as by birds.

Other names: Pope's head, barrel cactus, compass plant

Prickly pear, watjet
Opuntia dillenii

There are 250 species of *Opuntia* and most are built of flattened oval pads. Each pad grows at right angles to the one before it and the one after it. The fleshy pads are not the plant's leaves; they are segments of its stems. Pretty yellow flowers grow from the edges of the pads, usually in spring. When they drop off, small goblet-shaped fruits form. At first they are green, but when ripe they are a deep, dark red and good to eat. The best way to get rid of the prickles is to peel the fruits before eating them. In Mexico they are called tuna and the raw peeled fruits are rolled in sugar.

Prickly pears are the preferred food of cochineal insects which were highly valued as a source of an intensely red dye before carbon-based dyes were discovered. Just as mulberries are grown for silk worms, fields of prickly pears were grown to feed cochineal insects.

Prickly pears can be pestiferous. Like most cactuses they are natives of the Americas and have only recently been spread to the dry parts of Europe and Asia.

They were exported to Australia and threatened to take over the countryside before they were brought under control. The contents of the fleshy pads are used herbally for sore throats and applied to sores and skin infections. It is also used as a shampoo.

Organ pipe cactus
Cephalocereus royenii

Organ pipe cactuses are tall, light green and usually branch near the base. All the stems are vertical and have eight to ten ribs, each with an uninterrupted row of formidable spines. The spines can penetrate flip flops and sneakers easily. Look for birds' nests in these cactuses where they are safe from snakes and mongooses.

Silk cotton tree
Ceiba pentandra

The silk cotton tree often grows to be over 75 feet high and is one of the most dramatic trees on the islands, but it is not always the most popular. It is commonly called the devil's tree, but the reason for this is far from clear. In Dominica the tree is thought to house spirits, and its kapok, which elsewhere is considered the best stuffing for pillows, is not used because the spirits will disturb one's sleep. According to legend,

the spirits are absent between March and May and this is when the wood should be cut. If you ask why this tree is called the devil's tree, you may get a different answer every time. Some say it is because of the big thorns on the young trunks; others think that canoes made from the wood have a habit of coming to a bad end; another is sure that it is because the flowers attract hundreds of spooky bats.

The pinkish flowers, pollinated by bats, open about 15 minutes after sunset, in winter, when the tree is leafless. Bees clean up any remaining nectar early the next morning. After pollination, the seeds develop in pods, where light fluff cushions them and acts as parachutes to carry them on the wind. This silk cotton, better known as kapok, is the tree's most important product.

Kapok is a short lustrous fiber with many uses. Each fiber is a single air-filled cell with a waxy coating. It is eight times as light as cotton and five times as buoyant as cork. It is long lasting and not attacked by fungi or rodents. Life preservers have been made from it because it absorbs very little water after being afloat for a long time. Because it has low thermal conductivity and is an excellent sound absorber, it has been used in airplanes. It has great resiliency and is used for stuffing mattresses and sleeping bags. Kapok used to be considered unsuitable for spinning unless it was mixed with other fibers, but a method for spinning it has been found and it can now be made into yarn and cloth.

Silk cotton trees are native to the West Indies, as well as to much of the rest of

Frangipani caterpillar

66

Gumbo limbo

tropical America and to Africa. They are fast growing and thrive in either dry or wet situations, but they require full sunlight. The massive straight trunk has large buttresses at the base and rises branchless to a considerable height. The young trunk and branches are spiny and green, turning spineless and gray with age. The green bark can photosynthesize, thus bringing in a little extra income when the leaf factories are shut down in the dry season to conserve water. The branches are horizontal and often are strewn with epiphytes and vines. These stand out clearly when the trees are leafless. The leaves are on long leaf stalks and have from five to nine leaflets, radiating from a point.

Silk cotton wood is brittle and not very durable. Because of this, the trees often are left when timber is harvested. It has been used for coffins, carvings and dugout canoes.

The name *Ceiba* may have come from an old word for canoe. Sometimes the leaves are used for fodder. An oil can be pressed from the seeds and is used for lamp oil and for making soap. A respected herbalist from St. Lucia prescribes the leaves of this tree, saying "It keeps you from doing nothing."

Other names: devil's tree, fromager, mapou, mapou rouge, kapokier, pin tree. fonmaje

Kannik
Caesalpinia bonduc

Warri is the oldest known board game in the world and is played with the seeds of kannik. The plant and the game came to the West Indies from the Gold Coast where "warri" means house.

Kannik is a scrambling shrub or vine whose stems grow to 25 feet long. The leaves and stems are covered with vicious prickles and the seed pod is a miniature porcupine. The seedpod contains one or two large smooth gray seeds which, when taken out, will clack together like stones. Unlike stones, they float, and this plant is often found in the dry zone above beaches. The seeds are washed from place to place by the sea.

Kannik seeds, roasted until black and put into rum, are used herbally for gas or colds.

Other names: gray nickerbean, warri , canique grise, grey nicker, horse-nicker,

67

Bahama braziletto, konik, gwu sak borik, gwenzye bonwikt, z'yeux a chatte, kach kach.

Balsam
Croton flavens

There are many shrubs in the genus *Croton*. These are not related to the cultivated shrubs with weirdly-colored leaves whose common name is croton.

The name balsam is used for many crotons and most of them have a highly aromatic sap. Smell a handful of crushed leaves and you might think you are in a spice shop, but it is more likely that you are in a dry, over-grazed area where none but balsam can make a living. Balsam is unpalatable and takes over where other species have been eaten by cows or goats.

In addition to the smell, balsam can be recognized by its fuzzy leaves, which are used to scour pots. Old balsam leaves turn bright orange before they are shed, which can also help you recognize these shrubs. Just a few leaves are orange at any one time. The twiggy branches make fine brooms, usually to sweep the yard, rather than the house. Sap squeezed from the leaves is used to heal cuts.

Other names: sage, broom plant.

Fiddlewood
Citharexylum spinosum

This tree has good reliable wood and the French colonists called it "bois fidele," in appreciation of this attribute. A later English colonist, whose French was a little unreliable, gave it its Latin name *Citharexylum,* which means fiddlewood.

The hard, strong and dependable wood is used for furniture and construction and it makes durable fence posts.

The leafstalks are pink to orange, and make it easy to identify the tree. The brown twigs are four-sided. Small, sweet smelling white flowers are borne on upright spikes and are visited by bees. As the fruits mature, the flower stalks begin to droop under the weight of the berries. These are green at first, changing to orange and, finally, black. Each fruit contains two nutlets which each have two seeds. They are sweet tasting and probably a good food source for birds. Fiddlewood grows from southern Florida to Venezuela and withstands dry conditions very well.

It is used herbally for asthma. The leaves are pounded to extract juice and this is mixed with olive oil and drunk.

Other names: pendula, cutlet, bois cocklet, koklet, figbush, fairy tree, bois carre.

Frangipani
Plumeria alba

The wild frangipani is always white flowered, shading to yellow at the center. Its cousin, *Plumeria rubra*, has been invited into tropical gardens and is loved for the wonderful scent its waxlike pink or white flowers give off, especially at night. The blossoms are slow to wilt and are often used in decorations.

The slightly less fragrant wild frangipani is at home in the bush, far from hotel lights and gardeners. Its soft fat twigs hold needed water during the dry season and make it easy to identify. They are sparsely dressed with leaves and when the leaves fall -- which they usually do in the dry season -- obvious leaf scars are left on the stem. If cut, the stems exude copious poisonous milky sap. The leaves are much narrower than those of cultivated frangipanis, and are wrinkled as though they were sewn together with thread that shrank. The edges of the leaves are turned under, a common phenomenon of drought-adapted plants. Frangipani trees are small, usually not more than 15 feet high.

Sometimes, just before they would fall at the beginning of the dry season, the leaves are all eaten by big, colorful frangipani caterpillars *(Pseudosphinx tetrio)*. These insects can break down the toxic sap and they become toxic themselves in the process. Their bold yellow and black stripes tell birds to go eat something else. The same caterpillars also feed on allamandas, which are in the same family (Apocynaceae) and contain similar toxins. The caterpillars eat leaves until they are as fat as a little finger and five or six inches long. When they look as though they are just about to burst, they drop to the ground and bury themselves in soft earth to pupate, emerging as large silvery-gray hawk moths.

Frangipani trees can easily be grown from cuttings, but contrary to what you are supposed to do with most cuttings, it is necessary that they be dried out for a day or two before they are planted in dryish soil. If this is not done, they are likely to rot.

Sea island cotton
Gossypium barbadense

There are two cotton species in the islands, Sea island cotton and upland cotton *(Gossypium hirsutum)*, but both are quite variable and their geographic ranges meet in the Lesser Antilles. Here they have hybridized and it is not easy to tell who is who. Cotton is grown world-wide and has been used by people for over 3000 years; the Arawaks used it before Europeans came to the Caribbean. It is not known just how the different cotton species made their way around the world, but ocean currents may have helped. Some wild cottons have hard seeds that can float for a year in sea water.

Cotton is a small shrub with three to five-lobed leaves. The bell-shaped flowers have yellow petals with a brown dot at the base inside. The petals turn pink as they age. Three bracts surround the flower and they have a fringe of long teeth. The seed capsule splits into four parts and the cotton, which is tightly packed around the seeds, fluffs out. From a distance the cotton balls look like big white flowers.

Sea island cotton has the finest, longest-fibered cotton. Growing and spinning

this species was an important industry on Montserrat until recently. Now you will find it in the dry areas which are its natural habitat. Cotton is a sun-loving plant and won't tolerate shade. It can tolerate poor soil and invades impoverished abandoned fields.

Ancient cottons were perennials and they attracted a disreputable hoard of insects and diseases that persisted year after year. Humans have propagated annual forms. On these varieties room and board for pests is not available during some months of the year and the pests are starved out.

The flower bud of cotton is used herbally to treat earaches. The bud is warmed and its juice is squeezed into the ear.

Other names: cotonnier, coton, cotonnie, coton-pays.

Logwood
Haematoxylum campech- ianum

Logwood was introduced to the islands from Mexico and at one time was an important source of dye. The heartwood is a beautiful red color, and when chipped and boiled, makes an intense and extremely permanent black dye.

Logwood is a shrubby small tree with rough gray bark. It grows along roadsides and tolerates drought and poor soils. If you are near a logwood when it flowers, the rich and enticing smell will lead you to the tree. Honeybees will be there before you. They seek it out and make a delicious honey from the nectar. Logwoods are in bloom mostly from December to May. The hanging clusters of yellow flowers are one to three inches long and there are many small flowers in each cluster. The flat, oblong seedpods don't really stand out from the leaves when they are young and green. Later they turn brown and papery and stay on the tree for several months.

The wood has been used for furniture and posts and it makes high quality charcoal and firewood.

Other names: campeche, campeachy wood, kampech, champish.

West Indian creeper
Wedelia trilobata

This cheerful yellow daisy-like flower grows wild and has also been cultivated. It makes an excellent low maintenance lawn and will spread by way of roots that grow from horizontal stems. The flowers are borne singly, on slender stems that rise above the leaves. They have about ten ray florets (these are the outer florets that look like petals) and about 25 disk florets, the ones that make up the center of the flower. The leaves are variable but most often are toothed.

Wedelia is used herbally for a number of complaints. Together with portulaca, it is used for hemorrhaging in women and after childbirth a tea is made from it to clear the placenta. It is part of a herbal mixture for inflammation or when urine contains blood.

Other names: yellow marigold, verven caribe, herb soleil, vin vin caribe.

Logwood

BIRDS

Black-faced grassquit
Tiaris bicolor

Although grassquits are found in nearly every habitat, they are most abundant in acacia and cactus scrub, where perches and grass and weed seeds are readily available. Black-faced grassquits are quite tame and often approach people closely. They are sociable and spend both day and night in flocks. The males spend much time singing, if a buzzy dik-zee-zee-zee can be called singing.

Grassquits are only about four and a

half inches long. The head and breast of the male is dull black, the upper parts are a dull olive green and the lower parts are a pale olive color. The female and immature birds are more uniformly dirty olive green, though somewhat lighter below.

These little birds nest in trees or bushes, building a nest of grasses and other soft plant material. The entrance is at the side, possibly to shield the young from heat-sensing snakes.

Other names: grass bird, sparrow.

Tropical mocking-bird
Mimus gilvus

This bird can be found in the southern islands from Guadeloupe to Grenada. It won't make itself quite as quickly known as the other birds mentioned, but tropical mockingbirds are commonly seen in settled areas. Both sexes are about ten inches long, with gray heads and upper parts, dark wings edged with white and long blackish tails, conspicuously tipped with white. The underparts are creamy white and the birds are more or less gray on the throat and breast. There is a black stripe through the eye and a white stripe over the eye. The tropical mockingbird eats insects, berries, fruits and is fond of hot peppers. They have been known to eat the eggs of other birds.

They nest throughout the year, though mainly in the dry season. This bird has an extremely varied and musical song. A typical burst lasts several seconds and includes whistled notes of different pitches. It will also cluck, wheeze and make a sharp metallic "cheer" when alarmed. It occasionally mimics other species. Tropical mockingbirds are fiercely territorial, defending their territory from other birds, lizards, mongooses and even dogs.

Caribbean elaenia
Elaenia martinica

Elaenias are very common members of the flycatcher group and the Caribbean elaenia is the most widespread, occurring everywhere except in dense rainforest, but most at home in open areas with scattered trees. It is a grey unremarkable bird, with a prominent crest, white wing bars, a light gray belly and darker gray back. In St. Vincent and Grenada, the yellow-bellied elaenia is more common; a similar bird in most respects, except for its light yellow belly.

Like other flycatchers, elaenias dive bomb for insects from exposed perches. They vary their diet with seeds and fruits. They are active birds and are sometimes very talkative among themselves, beginning early in the morning before the other birds. Included in their scratchy notes is a raucous "che-up."

They nest in trees from 4 to 60 feet above the ground, making a tidy cup of fine vegetation which is sometimes bound with spider silk and lined with feathers.

Other names: pee whistler, siffleur, jui blanco.

Smooth billed ani, mel kobo
Crotophaga ani

Ani feathers have a nice shine to them. These clannish birds are almost coal black, with some bronze iridescence on the head and neck and heavy parrot-like bills. They have long tails, short rounded wings and are not particularly adept at flying. A long wobbling glide precedes an ani landing. They often hang around cattle, picking up grasshoppers and other insects that the cattle have disturbed. Anis also feed on fruits and berries in fields and open areas, but they are rarely seen in the forest.

They are in the cuckoo family, a group with its own ideas about family values. There are some cuckoos that any American politician would approve of, but European cuckoos incline towards laying their eggs in other birds' nests, and in the ani branch of the family, they usually build communal nests. Several pairs will cooperate in building a single nest. The females lay eggs -- as many as 26, but more often 10 to 15-- and all the adults share in incubating the eggs and raising the young.

ANIMALS

Ground lizard
Ameiva ameiva

When the small land area of the islands of the West Indies is taken into account, the population of reptiles, especially lizards, is extremely rich. There are many lizard species and some of them exist only on one island. There are 19 lizards in the genus Ameiva alone, usually called ground lizards. Ground lizards are not only diverse, they are also a successful group and you can't walk very far in most islands before you will hear rustling in the dry leaves. If you sit quietly, a ground lizard may emerge. Many are brown and often they have stripes. The males of some species have bright blue stripes. Ground lizards do not have dewlaps, the expandable throat pouches that distinguish the tree lizards, nor can they change color. They do not climb trees, but they will climb rocks. As lizards go, ground lizards are quite active foragers.

Most lizards are low-energy animals. The daily energy expenditure of birds and small mammals, adjusted for size, is 20 to 40 times greater than that of lizards. The lizard lifestyle has its advantages. They can survive on very little food and they convert more of this food into lizard, as opposed to frittering it away by flying or running around all day.

From our exalted mammalian point of view, reptiles have complex and peculiar hearts which are not capable of supplying well-oxygenated blood at the high rates and pressures that we enjoy. Thus they can sustain only low levels of aerobic activity (the kind that uses oxygen directly). In addition, aerobic activity is temperature dependent, which further limits its usefulness to these cold-blooded animals. However, luckily for them, they have an alterna-

tive. Lizards can use anaerobic metabolic pathways which are far less temperature-dependent and which allow the lizard to indulge in impressive short term performance -- either chasing an insect or fleeing from a predator. This, however, leaves a lizard exhausted, and its strategy is to scrupulously conserve energy, maintaining as large a reserve capacity as possible.

On most islands lizards are the commonest vertebrates. You may even see a large iguana, for these survive on several islands. World-wide, small lizards tend to be carnivores and the large ones (over 100 grams) are herbivores. Insects and other arthropods are abundant and make a hearty snack for a small lizard but they don't amount to much for a large lizard, even if it were fast enough to catch them. It is more efficient for large lizards to dine on plants, and iguanas become vegetarians during adolescence, just like all my nieces and nephews. Plants are abundant and don't run away. Large lizards are less vulnerable to predation (humans excepted) and they can bask in the hot sun, slowly heating and digesting their stomach contents. Look for an iguana in full sun, cooking the meal he has just eaten.

West Indian nasute-termites
Nasutitermes costalis

What is that large, dark brown, misshapen lump in a tree? Most likely a termite nest, also called a termitarium. Constructed out of digested wood, and cemented with glue made from termite feces, these basketball-sized nests usually are low in a bush or tree and brown tunnels radiate from them in all directions.

Like many ants and bees, termites are social insects with a complex division of labor. Termite workers, small and light in color are both male and female, unlike the female-only work force of the honeybee colony. They are blind and follow chemical trails. Only the queens and kings can reproduce and there is one king and one queen in a colony of many thousands of workers and soldiers. The queen is kept safe well inside the nest and is much bigger than the other colony members. She has such an enormous, egg-stuffed abdomen that she can barely move.

It is usually in June that winged termites are produced, and they leave the termitarium in great swarms. These males and females are potential kings and queens and can mate and begin new colonies.

Another common termite, the West Indian dry-wood termite (*Cryptotermes brevis*), lives in burrows excavated in wood and this species doesn't construct external nests.

The tiny termite, unlike most insects, can digest wood, but to do so it needs help from yet tinier organisms that live in its gut. These minute insects are so abundant that some scientists think the methane and carbon dioxide that they produce as by products contribute significantly to global warming.

Purple-clawed hermit crab, soldier crab
Coenobita clypeatus

It is common to see the shells of sea snails scrambling around in the branches of bushes and trees, often quite far from water, and looking very out of place. If you pick one up you will see the purple-clawed hermit crab, the most common crab of the dry forest. Well, what you will really see is its left front claw and some pincers, which have evolved to double as a sturdy front door, fitting the opening of the snail's shell. Land hermit crabs can be found as far as five miles inland and at altitudes up to 350 feet above sea level, but they must stay near enough to the sea to be able to return to lay their eggs. On some nights during the dry season hundreds of the adult crabs may be found on the shore in the splash zone,

where, at low tide, the females crawl to the water's edge or onto wet rocks to fling their hatching eggs into the sea.

This is a rugged little animal; it has two hefty claws, stout walking legs and short eye stalks, and, with its heavy adopted shell, is the most cumbersome of the land crabs. The front part is well protected but the abdomen is soft and vulnerable and ends with two hooks which attach it to the borrowed shell. When a crab outgrows its house, it must search for a new one. West Indian top snail (*Cittarium pica*) shells are highly preferred. But before exposing its tender abdomen, a hermit crab will explore a prospective new home with its legs and feelers as thoroughly as possible. If, after long deliberations, the crab decides to move, the act is almost instantaneous. Sometimes the new house doesn't live up to expectations and there are stories of frustrated hermit crabs trying on house after house until exhaustion overcomes them. Despite all the care these crabs appear to exercise, it is estimated that 50% of crab homicides occur while changing quarters. Their fellow crabs are both cannibalistic and in hot competition for the good shells. Where housing is in short supply, hollow plant stems and small bottles have been seen wandering around on the rocks.

Although this crab goes as far from the sea as any land crab and can use either fresh or salt water, it is in fact not as physiologically adapted to a terrestrial life as are many other land crabs. It depends upon keeping a reserve of water in its snail shell, a bit like a diver keeps a tank of air while under water. One scientist found that all the crabs found far from the sea were equipped with close-fitting shells. Those with sloppy fitting shells, from which water could evaporate, were restricted to seaside habitats.

The purple-clawed hermit is not choosy about its food and, as well as eating its fellow crabs, will feed on a variety of plants, including the poisonous manchineel, or on carrion, feces or dog food. The soft body of the hermit crab is used as fish bait, but not for food.

©Katie Shears

Plants

1. Norfolk Island pine
2. Bougainvillea
3. Oleander
4. Pride of Barbados
5. Royal palm
6. Hibiscus
7. Ixora
8. African tulip tree
9. Flamboyant
10. Red ginger
11. Purple allamanda
12. Yellow allamanda
13. Anthurium

Birds

14. Lesser Antillean bullfinch
15. Carib grackle
16. Bananaquit
17. Doctorbird
18. Green-throated Carib

Animals

19. Tree lizard

Caribbean people come from many ethnic backgrounds and are highly individualistic when it comes to ideas, politics, and gardens. Almost everyone has a garden and space will be found for flowers on even the smallest plot of land surrounding a house. At the other end of the scale are the large formal gardens, approached by long tree-lined drives, with trimmed lawns and carefully laid out flower beds.

Fruit trees are often included for their obviously practical benefits and vegetables are sometimes grown among the flowers. In towns, window boxes, flower pots and even large tin cans are planted with cheerful blossoms.

Some people have a laissez-faire attitude, doing the least possible to keep their land from reverting to bush. Others go to great pains to keep everything meticulously tidy, often covering flower beds with the dark brown husks of nutmeg to stop weeds from coming up.

Plants make a good substitute for clothes lines, and the weekly wash is often draped across hedges and shrubs. The sharp, long spines of plants in the agave family can quickly convert a t-shirt into something with enough arm holes to suit an octopus. Some deal with this by covering each spine with a whole, carefully blown egg shell, creating very strange eggplants.

Gardens in full sun are often the most exuberantly colorful, with flamboyant trees and bougainvillea providing vivid splashes of purple, orange and red. Anthuriums and ginger do better in a more moist and shaded environment.

Some flowers have been in cultivation for so long that their origins are lost. Others have changed very little since being plucked from the wild and transported to tropical countries around the world. Still others are the recent result of intensive work by horticulturists. The job of creating new plant varieties takes dedication, skill, patience, a tiny pollinating brush and a great deal of luck.

The tropical gardener has many choices, and flowers succeed by competing for his attention. If beautiful and not too demanding, they get planted and nurtured; their competitors are kept in check by a cutlass. The gardener can choose plants from all over the world and only a handful of the flowers you will see are native species. Most plants flower seasonally, with a preference for the dry season, but whatever the time of year, something is at its peak.

PLANTS

Flamboyant
Delonix regia

A visitor in June cannot help but notice the dazzlingly bright red flowers of the flamboyant tree, which is frequently planted in towns as well as in gardens. The winter visitor will notice the seed pods. At first these are green but they turn brown when mature and grow to an impressive two feet long. The seeds become loose inside the pods and they make a distinctive rattle, making the pods popular as shack shacks (rattles).

The tree is a native of Madagascar and its generous shady umbrella shape, along with its glorious blossoms, have made it a favorite throughout the islands. One flamboyant leaf consists of about 500 small leaflets, arranged on 10 to 25 pinnae (subdivisions of the leaf stalk). The tree is well adapted to drought and loses its leaves during the dry season. It flowers at the very end of the dry season. A local farmer told me that he watches for the flowering of the flamboyant for it signals the coming of the rains.

Other names: poinciana, flame tree.

Bougainvillea

African tulip tree
Spathodea campanulata

The African tulip tree is another showy, red-flowered tree. It is a native of Africa and it, too, can be seen in many parks and gardens. The one to two foot long dark green compound leaves have 11 to 19 leaflets, and they stay on the tree year round. Tulip trees flourish in direct sun but do not tolerate quite such dry conditions as the flamboyant. They flower year round, but the flowers are most abundant from late winter to early summer. The flower clusters are large, about four inches long and three inches across. They are usually held high in the crown of the tree. The flower buds are curious: they are filled with stinky water which squirts out when they are squeezed, so they double as free, disposable water pistols for kids. The open, empty seed pods look like toy boats. But, alas, soon after launching, they close again to become sodden pontoons.

Other name: flame of the forest.

Norfolk Island pine
Araucaria heterophylla

Norfolk Island pines are neat and orderly. The trees have evenly spaced branches and are shaped like tidy pyramids. They are used as Christmas trees in some islands and, from a distance, they look just like plastic Christmas trees. They aren't plastic, but they aren't pines, either. They don't have needles, but their leaves, which curve in and overlap each other along the stem, do a good job of imitating needles. Sixty million year old fossils of plants in this family are commonly found and they are among the oldest conifers that have survived to the present.

Norfolk Island pines are grown as houseplants in the north. In the tropics they can grow to 200 feet high and are planted for lumber as well as to accent lawns and gardens. Most of the leaves drop off in the dry season.

Royal palm
Roystonea regia

Most palms are beautiful, but the clean lines of the royal palm make it the most elegant of them all: a designer palm.

You are most likely to see it in formal gardens or lining the approach to a large estate house. It distinguishes itself by its stately shape. The smooth gray trunk usually bulges at the base and then bulges again part way up, giving the appearance of a very slim vase. The leaf bases form a long smooth green extension which is topped with giant featherlike leaves. This fast growing Caribbean tree is from Cuba and reaches a height of about 70 feet. Like the coconut palm, the leaves are used for thatching. The oily seeds have been used to fatten pigs and chickens.

Bougain-villea
Bougain-villea spectabilis

Bougainvillea is probably the first flower you will see. It forms great mounds, sprawls upwards into the trees and onto roofs or can be trimmed as a polite little hedge. It flowers prodigiously and comes in most colors of the rainbow. Many varieties are startlingly bright and almost glow in late afternoon light. They are always in flower, but the flowers are most abundant during the dry season. Such a magnificent display -- how do they manage it? Some may be surprised to learn that bougainvillea has no petals. The colorful parts are modified leaves, called bracts, which are longer lasting than petals. They provide advertising for a series of small petal-less flowers which are produced inside the bracts over a long period of time. Not only is bougainvillea excessively colorful, it is also exceptionally tough. It tolerates drought, poor soil, heavy pruning and the confined life of a houseplant in the north.

Bougainvillea spectabilis, the first popular bougainvillea, was red, but now many other species are known and horticulturists have persuaded them to supply us with pink, orange, mauve and white flowers. Bougainvillea is a native of Brazil and is named after Louis de Bougainville, a French navigator who took it home in 1768.

Travelers tree, travelers palm
Ravenala madagascariensis

This peculiar relative of the banana stands as tall as a tree and its leaves form a giant flat fan. The 10- to 15-foot long leaves flare from the top of a palm-like trunk.

Travelers tree is from Madagascar and got its name because the wide sheaths at the base of the leaves hold water. If you don't object to drinking the occasional drowned insect, you can poke a hole at the base of a leaf and collect up to a quart of liquid. It is often said that the fans always face north or south, but this is not true.

Yellow allamanda
Allamanda cathartica

Allamanda is another beauty from Brazil. The showy, fragrant, clear yellow flowers have got them where they are today -- in nearly every garden in the tropics. But the exquisite glowing reddish brown buds of allamanda would win it a place in my garden, even if they never opened. The shiny leaves and tidy shape of this shrub add to its appeal, but there are also forms which climb. A toxic milky sap protects the plants from most insects, but they are sometimes

attacked by a voracious caterpillar (*Pseudosphinx tetrio*), an enemy they share with their relative, the frangipani.

Purple allamanda
Cryptostegia grandiflora

This plant, originally from Africa and Madagascar, is most often called purple allamanda, although it is not related to the allamandas. (There is a real purple allamanda, *Allamanda violacea*.) This false purple allamanda is superficially a dead ringer for allamanda, and even has similar toxic milky sap, which has given it another name, rubber vine. Rubber has been made commercially from the sap. You often see rubber vine growing vigorously by the side of the road. If you find a seed pod that has turned brown and hard, strip off the husk and you will find that the seed pod is pointed like a pen nib. School children sometimes use these as pens.

Other names: rubber vine, pen plant.

Hibiscus
Hibiscus rosa-sinensis

The hibiscus is the show-off in a large flashy family. Some varieties have enormous flowers, up to seven inches across, with five petals and a curious protruding column. The column looks like a small bottle brush and it holds both the male and female flower parts. The stamens (the pollen-producing male parts) are the bristles at the sides of the brush. The five-parted stigma (the female receptacle for pollen grains) is at the end of the brush.

You wouldn't think a flower so beautiful would have to earn a living, but hibiscus is also called shoe flower because you can use it to polish your shoes -- if they are black. And the leaves, when pounded with water, make a passable shampoo.

This garden hibiscus is believed to have originated in tropical Asia, but it is no longer found in the wild. The genus includes many trees and shrubs, several of which are native to the Caribbean.

Red ginger
Alpinia purpurata

This handsome native of the Pacific Islands is another favorite flower which, in reality, is not a flower at all. As with bougainvillea, its red showy "petals" are really bracts. These modified leaves stay in good condition for a far longer time than most mere petals. The true flowers are tiny, white and ephemeral. You will catch one now and again. The seeds often germinate while still within the bracts and the small plants tumble to the ground when the bracts disintegrate.

This is not the true ginger of ginger snaps, but is closely related to it and the root looks and smells like ginger. Ginger leaves are distinctive: long and elliptical, with almost no leaf stalk, they are pinnately veined (like a feather) and can easily be distinguished from lilies which have parallel veins.

Anthurium
Anthurium andraeanum

It is ironic that the makers of plastic flowers strive and strive to make their creations look like real flowers. In the anthurium we have a real flower that has succeeded in looking just like a plastic one. Anthuriums are the largest genus in the aroid family. When you look at an anthurium, you see a good looking, bushy, tail-like appendage that would do credit to the rear end of a small mammal. Indeed, the name anthurium means "tail flower" and the tiny flowers of the plant are clustered around this tail, which is called a spadix. The flowers, however, are small and not showy enough to attract pollinators, so the anthurium uses an eye-catching bract, often of brilliant color, which sits just underneath the spadix. A bract which surrounds a spadix is called a spathe. Again, this modified leaf lasts longer than a true flower, making it popular for flower arrangements.

Most aroid flowers emit foul-smelling odors to attract beetles and flies which then pollinate them. Not so the anthurium. It produces sweet nectar and is visited by bees and even hummingbirds.

Pride of Barbados
Caesalpinia pulcherrima

Pride of Barbados does so well in the West Indies that it frequently escapes from the garden to the roadside, where it thrives as well on its own as it does under supervision. The bright orange flowers, often edged in yellow, are at the top of the shrub. Beneath them are seed pods, in various stages of development. Mature seed pods are a dark, dark brown and seem coarse and gloomy compared to the delicate bright flowers and feathery foliage.

The origins of this plant are a little shadowy. It may be a West Indian native or it may have come from Mexico or central America.

Other names: dwarf poinciana, flower fence.

Ixora
Ixora coccinea

The original Indian ixora was red. Now there are orange, yellow, pink and white ixoras as well. In the clusters of four-petalled flowers, the unopened buds stick out beyond the opened flowers. The opposite leaves are not particularly distinctive, but ixora flowers year round and not many common garden plants have four equal

Allamanda with royal palms in the background

petals, spread like a Maltese cross. In India the flowers, bark and leaves are all used medicinally. Ixoras adjust well to being clipped as hedges.

Oleander, Rosebay
Nerium oleander

Several species from the dogbane family (Apocynaceae) are common in gardens. The three most popular, frangipani, allamanda, and oleander are all toxic. Pliny, who died in 79 AD, called attention to oleander's poisonous properties. It is so deadly that meat cooked on skewers made from the twigs can be lethal. In spite of this, it has been used medicinally for heart failure and dropsy.

Oleanders are upright shrubs or small trees with narrow leaves which have a noticeable midrib. The satiny five-petalled flowers are most often in the pink to purple range, but occasionally are yellow or white. Oleanders love heat and sun, and withstand dry periods well.

Poinsettia
Euphorbia pulcherrima

Remember that poinsettia you got for Christmas and struggled to keep alive while it exhibited less and less interest in life, the more things you tried? Here, by comparison, they are irrepressible, growing to 15 feet high, with dense crowns of brilliant red bracts.

Yes, again the true flowers are tiny things buried in the bright scarlet. One of the reasons your poinsettia may have lost its color in spring is that flowering stops when day length increases. Since in the tropics most days are never much more than 12 hours long, poinsettias bloom for much of the year.

You may notice a smaller shrub covered in white flowers. At first glance it looks nothing like poinsettia, but a closer inspection reveals that the "flowers" are

Anthuriums

83

little white miniature poinsettias. It is *Euphorbia leucocephala* (white-headed) usually called Christmas bush or snow on the mountains.

The genus Euphorbia contains over 2000 species and they are so different from each other that it makes us wonder about botanists. Some tiny low-growing weeds as well as giant cactus-like trees of the African desert are included in the same genus as poinsettias. The flower structures, on which botanical classifications are based, all are similarly configured: a female flower is surrounded by several males.

BIRDS

Doctorbird
Orthorhyncus cristatus
The doctorbird is not only the most common hummingbird, but also one of the most common of all birds in the islands. You will find this busy feathered helicopter in every habitat. Flowers are its bread and butter, so gardens attract a good number of them. The male has a noticeable green or blue-green crest. The female is paler green on the back and light gray or brown below and her crest is not conspicuous.

Hummingbirds feed primarily on nectar. They visit, and at the same time pollinate, many different flowers. Their long thin beaks probe into the deepest flowers and they hover right at the entrance to the flower while they feed.

Flowers which are pollinated by birds and bats must supply a lot more nectar than insect-pollinated flowers because these big warm-blooded pollinators require more energy. However, it becomes important to keep that expensive nectar out of the probosces of insects which are too small to touch the right parts and effect pollination. For this reason hummingbird-pollinated flowers tend to have long flower necks which are only accessible to long slender beaks. They don't have the wonderful fragrance that attracts insects (and humans), because birds don't respond very much to smell. And they are often red, a color most insects don't see, but one which is an excellent signal to birds. From the flower's perspective, it is worth putting out extra sugar, for hummingbirds cover a larger area than most insects and can cross-pollinate flowers that are a considerable distance apart.

Like other hummingbirds, the flying ability of doctorbirds is dazzling. They can hover in one spot and dart off in any direction at high speed. From 22% to 34% of a hummingbird's total body weight is in flight muscles.

These are feisty little birds, given to jealously guarding their food sources, and they often engage in dramatic aerial chases. The female builds a thimble-sized nest which she lines with spider webs or milkweed fluff. Two tiny white eggs are laid between February and July and are incubated by the female. The young are cared for by the female, too. The males -- well, they are more brightly colored.

Other names: Antillean crested hummingbird, frou frou.

Green-throated carib
Sericotes holosericeus
Another hummingbird, the green-throated carib, also frequents gardens, as well as dry woodlands and agricultural lands. It is all green except for some violet on the breast and a dark tail. The green-throated carib is larger than the doctorbird. Their nesting and feeding habits are similar.

The startling colors seen in hummingbirds are called structural colors, as they are caused by the physical structure of the feathers and not by pigments, like most colors. The feathers reflect and absorb light to create color in the same way that light scattered by an oil slick can produce all the colors of the rainbow. These colors depend on the proper light angle to be visible; otherwise the bright areas appear black.

In spite of their high-speed lives, hummingbirds live for a long time. A green-throated carib that was captured as an adult lived in captivity for ten and a half years.

Other names: green doctorbird, colibri vert.

Bananaquit
Coereba flaveola

This tame and cheerful little bird is everywhere. It is flexible about both food and habitat and so does well both in gardens and among crops. Bananaquits even feed on cecropia fruits in the rainforest. Some of their feeding methods are ingenious. They can perch or hang upside down and in flower gardens can be seen stealing nectar by poking a hole at the base of large flowers, in flagrant disobedience of the pollination pact between flowers and nectar eaters. They do approach most flowers in the conventional way, sipping up nectar with their slender curved bills. If nectar is scarce, they can do well on a diet of insects or they will pierce fruits and suck up the juice. They may come to your tea party and eat sugar from the table.

Bananaquits are only four inches long, very active and often vocal, calling with wheezy squeaks. They often form noisy small groups. Males and females look alike and the ones you are most likely to see are easily recognized by a bright yellow belly and back. On some islands there is just a yellow-green wash on the breast and the rest is black. Head, wings and tail are almost black and each eye has a bright white stripe over it.

Bananaquits always seem to be building a nest. An untidy globe-shaped nest is woven from grasses and narrow leaves by both members of a pair. When not breeding, they build even messier roosting nests in which they sleep singly. All their nests have side entrances, perhaps to avoid detection by snakes. They sometimes nest in a big prickly cactus to avoid predation by the mongoose. Bananaquits have an extended breeding season, with multiple clutches each year of two or three heavily spotted eggs. Only the female incubates the eggs but both parents feed the young.

After they leave the nest, the fledglings may spend nights roosting in the nests of other birds until they are able to build their own roosts.

The bananaquit is the only species in its family, but there are more than 30 races, a testimony to the adaptability of this bird.

Other names: sugar bird, chibi chibi.

Carib grackle
Quiscalis lugubris

You will not have to go and look for this bold medium-sized bird. It is just as likely to come and look for you, especially if you are eating outside. It will hover around your table, looking for an opportunity to grab a scrap of food. If you get up and walk away, it will take your place without a second thought. Males are black with a purple sheen and a bright light yellow eye. Their tails are trough- or boat-shaped, but the female's tail is flat. She is also much duller. Female grackles vary in color from island to island. In some places they are nearly black; on other islands they are pale brown above and nearly white on the chest and belly.

Carib grackles are found on all islands. They are most abundant in cleared and settled areas, where they do well on garbage, scraps and leftovers. They flock together, roosting and nesting together high up in tall trees where the females lay three to five pale blue eggs. They nest in all months of the year. They have an unmistakable rich two note call, loud enough to wake you out of a deep sleep. If you use a little imagination, you can hear "Bequia sweet."

Other names: Bequia sweet, Vincent chupit, blackbird, cha cha, plenty-better bird.

Lesser Antillean bullfinch, red breast
Loxigilla noctis

The Lesser Antillean bullfinch is a small bird, but is almost as bold as the grackle. The male has shiny black feathers and a bright red patch under his chin. The females and immature birds are plainer, all gray or brown. They

African tulip tree

seem to seek out buildings for nest sites. Hanging plants, light fixtures and shrubs in hotel lobbies are considered desirable bullfinch lodgings. Despite having the classic seed-cracking beak which is a characteristic of the finch family, they have a weakness for sugar. As with most flocking birds, there is a lot of quarreling and scolding among bullfinches.

Ginger

ANIMALS

Tree lizard, zandoli *Anolis aeneus* The garden is a good place to keep your eyes open for lizards, especially tree lizards. They are in the genus *Anolis*, a very successful group which includes over 100 species in the West Indies alone. No one species lives on the whole island chain, but several, including *Anolis aeneus*, can be found on several islands.

These are the lizards sold in pet shops as chameleons, renowned for their ability to change color. Anoles may change color for two reasons: to change temperature or for camouflage. Being cold blooded, anoles depend on heat from the environment to get them going in the morning. They begin the day a dark color and bask in the sun to absorb needed heat. By mid day, after a few forays for insects, they can get too hot. Then their skin lightens and they reflect unwanted heat. At other times, when a lizard is comfortably warm, it will change color to match the branch or leaf that it is sitting on.

All male anoles have rounded sacs under their necks which are called dewlaps. Anoles are territorial and the dewlaps are inflated as a threatening signal to other males. The display is made more obvious by an up and down motion, as though the animal were doing push ups. If you watch a male indulging in this behavior and look around, you may see another male responding in kind. This display often results in a furious chase, ending when the interloper gets shown off the territory. Anoles climb trees and generally live on a varied arthropod diet of cockroaches, crickets, ants, spiders, scorpions, grasshoppers, insect larvae and mosquitos as well as worms and land snails, shell and all. They will also eat bread, spaghetti, ripe bananas, mangos, sugar, the occasional hummingbird egg and baby tree lizards.

This latter habit makes it tough to be a baby tree lizard, and the young ones have to seek out a territory out of the way of their elders. The species *Anolis aeneus* was studied in Grenada, where hatchlings emerge from August through December, weighing about as much as a postage stamp. Larger tree lizards are not their only worry; other predators include carib grackles, snakes and mockingbirds. Since adult tree lizards prefer the shade, the juveniles seek out clearings to avoid getting eaten. Rather than striking out and looking for new territory, they look for areas next door to other baby tree lizards, as this is a sign that the area meets lizard requirements. They stake out a small territory of about two square feet. When a maturing tree lizard gets big enough to take its chance among the big boys in the shade, there will

often be a fight for its vacated lot. Growth rates are highly variable, depending on the availability of food, temperature and water. It takes at least nine months for a tree lizard to become mature. Females mature at one and a half inches, males at about two inches. When fully grown, even with their long tails, they reach only five or six inches. As they grow, they shed their tissue-thin skin. It takes about two hours for a tree lizard to shed its skin, which it then eats.

House gecko
Hemi-dactylus mabouia

Don't be alarmed by the small plump lizards that come out at night. These are harmless geckos, the commonest of which is the house gecko or woodslave. They seek out buildings and are quite used to people. Many have traveled as stowaways on boats and the woodslave may have come to the Caribbean with slaves from Africa. Not many reptiles are active at night, because, being cold-blooded, most depend on the sun to warm them. The gecko's nocturnal habit may have evolved as a way to avoid daytime predators, such as birds. The warmth of tropical nights is enough to keep these little fellows going.

Geckos are excellent at keeping down all manner of creeping and flying house pests, even quite large ones. If a gecko catches a large active insect, it may subdue it by bashing it against a hard surface.

Geckos easily outdo Spiderman at crawling up vertical surfaces and across the ceiling, thanks to velcro-like feet. Their feet have flap-like scales which are edged with tiny hooks, called microvilli. These can grasp even the smallest irregularities, giving the mistaken impression that they are coated with something sticky. This in turn has led to the superstitious and completely false belief that a gecko can only be removed from human skin by killing it with a hot iron. Geckos don't want to be on people at all, and should one find itself so misplaced it will leave as soon as it can.

Geckos sometimes make strange clicking noises, highly unusual for a reptile. The female lays little round eggs with hard white shells which can be found behind books on bookshelves or in other dark corners. Geckos have short fat tails that they can drop off when attacked. After the tail drops off, it continues to wiggle to attract the attacker, allowing the remodeled gecko to beat a hasty retreat.

Other names: mabwya, woodslave.

© Katie Shears

Plants

1. West Indian mahogany
2. Calabash
3. Lion's tail
4. Tamarind
5. Annatto
6. Saman
7. Coralita
8. Castor bean
9. Sensitive plant
10. Woman's tongue
11. Leucaena
12. Lantana
13. Ginger Thomas

Birds

14. Zenaida dove
15. Common ground dove
16. Gray kingbird
17. Glossy cowbird

Animals

18. Mongoose

Wherever they live, humans change the landscape, molding it to their needs. Some changes are intentional, others are accidental. The roadside is a good place to look for some of these alterations.

Steel, shaped into a hoe, shovel, plow, or bulldozer, changes the entire economy of the plant community by opening areas of forest to light and exposing bare soil. Many of the native species which now are so common in this habitat probably played an insignificant role in pre-European times. These are plants that require a lot of light and are able to grow quickly on bare soil. Often called pioneer plants, they make big investments in small, light weight seeds. Before man, these seeds waited for an old tree to fall, and grew up in the sunlit opening. This was a relatively rare occurrence, and so were these plants. In a natural environment they are waifs, rarely getting a foothold. In man's footsteps they are kings.

Sometimes land by the roadside has been degraded by years of intensive sugar cane production, which has slowly robbed the soil of its nutrients, including nitrogen. In such soil, nitrogen fixing plants, many of which are in the legume family, often prevail. These plants have bacteria living in a close association with their roots. The bacteria take nitrogen from the air and make it available to the plant. Leaf litter from these plants contains this nutrient, and nitrogen fixing plants help restore the soil. On subfertile soils, legumes such as mimosas and acacias have a competitive advantage over other plants.

Many of the plants at the sides of the road are newcomers to the Caribbean and they have been imported from all corners of the earth. Like the native roadside plants, they can take advantage of the changes that people have wrought, and many have been in close association with us for millennia. Some of them were brought intentionally and others hitched a ride, arriving as seeds mixed in sacks of grain or among belongings.

In the course of the long association between these plants and people, people have come to divine their useful properties. There are plants that make good brooms and are used to sweep the yard, plants with fruits that make good bowls and cups, and plants that can be used to cure the ills of both body and mind.

Ethnobotany is the study of the relationship between humans and plants. Many of the plants used in folk remedies since time immemorial contain compounds that are important ingredients of modern medicines, and the search for new cures often uses herbal medicine as a starting point. Some herbal remedies are based simply on practical results that have been handed down from generation to generation. At other times, herbal medicine is mixed with ideas about spirits, curses and charms in a belief system known as obeah. Obeah is not exactly a religion, but it refers to spells and charms that can be imparted to people or their belongings. Herbs to break spells must be very carefully prepared. While obeah still exists in the islands, it is not the powerful force it once was. Still, many island people have at least a mild belief in such things, just as some Americans and Europeans knock on wood or furtively glance at their astrological predictions when reading the evening paper. Many plants that are used herbally contain compounds that are highly poisonous and "bush teas" have been known to kill as well as to cure.

Plants are not the only creatures affected by human presence. Birds which can take advantage of a changed habitat do very well. The glossy cowbird population may be increasing in part because these birds thrive in cleared land. Kingbirds have appropriated the telephone wires, and sally forth from them for insects. Doves often feed on bare ground and they are relatively unafraid of people. However, like their relative, the pigeon, they will keep a wary eye on you, perhaps realizing that you are capable of roasting and eating them.

Leucaena
Leucaena leucocephala

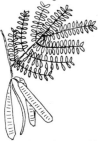

Leucaena (pronounced looseena) is native to the West Indies, but now it is far more common than in early times. It grows like a weed on cleared land and forms dense thickets. If cut back, new shoots will grow. You see it just about everywhere along the roadside and in abandoned fields as bushes, though if not cut back, it grows to be a sizable tree. It has a deep central taproot which helps in dry spells and it can fix atmospheric nitrogen, a help on poor soils. It is an untidy looking plant with many small leaflets and abundant thin flat pods. When young, the pods are green and can be used as a vegetable. Mature pods are brown, hang in bunches and contain a single row of glossy brown seeds. The seeds are pretty and are often strung as beads. The fluffy white balls are made up of many tiny flowers.

You may see a donkey laden with leucaena branches, but he isn't bringing home his own dinner. Leucaena is regarded as a high protein forage for cattle, sheep and goats and branches are cut and carried to the animals. But the leaves are dangerous for maned animals. The hair of donkeys, hogs, horses and mules will fall out if they eat leucaena. It can even kill these animals if they eat too much of it. Leucaena is sometimes called a miracle plant, for it can grow very fast. A tree can grow to 30 feet high in just three years and a leucaena holds the record for the most wood added to a tree in one year. It makes excellent charcoal. Charcoal is the most common cooking fuel in many Caribbean islands and fuelwood harvesting contributes significantly to deforestation. To offset this, leucaena is now being grown in plantations on many islands.

Other names: wild tamarind, wild mimosa, monval, tamarin batard, macata, macata-bourse.

Leucaena

Coralita with a tamarind tree behind

Coralita
Antigonon leptopus

This bright, rosy, weedy vine is out to cover the earth. Unchecked it will try to drape itself over almost the entire landscape, though you see it most often covering roadside hedges with a blanket of pretty pink flowers. As with many other plants, such as bougainvillea, the true flowers are hidden. What we admire are the five showy heart-shaped sepals. If you pry the sepals open, you can see eight yellow stamens. There are no petals. The leaves are also heart-shaped and they have wavy margins.

Once coralita is established, small tubers grow from the roots, deep in the ground. It is not admired at all by anyone who tries to get rid of it, for these tubers break off and grow new plants. It also produces abundant seeds. Herbalists make a tea from the leaves and flowers to treat coughs and throat restrictions. It is a member of the buckwheat family and a native of Mexico.

Other names: coral vine, la belle Mexicane, bride's tears, cemetary vine.

Sensitive plant
Mimosa pudica

On St. Kitts, in 1634, Father Andrew White recorded his first encounter with the sensitive plant: ". . . here is also the virgin plant, which they terme the sensible tree, which after the least touch of one's hand I see fall down withered, and then again revived after a little space."

Sensitive plant varies from a delicate low-growing weed along the roadside to a rampant, spiny, dominant plant in pastures. It has numerous small leaflets and the pink flowers are in balls, about a half inch in diameter.

Scientists hypothesize that the sensitive plant's fainting spells may have evolved to freak insects out. The leaves close extremely quickly for a plant, so quickly that they may even drop hungry insects to the ground, if they haven't fled in terror. You may enjoy imitating a hungry insect and watching the leaflets close up and the whole leaf drop down until the greenery is reduced to grayish sticks.

There are about 400 mimosa species and this one is native to South America. The stem and root are used herbally as an emetic and a purgative. The plant is also used if you fall and "your whole inside shake up."

Other names: scairdy plant, hontuese, honteuse femelle, maria honte, to mawi.

Life plant
Bryophyllum pinnatum

Life plant is originally from Madagascar, but is now widespread and has made itself at home around houses and alongside paths. The stems are reddish and both the stems and leaves are fleshy. The margins of the leaves are notched. The bell-like red and green flowers are on straight, tall flower stalks.

Life plant has many medicinal uses. The leaves can be warmed over a fire and applied directly for athlete's foot. The bruised leaves can be placed on the head to cure a headache. Life plant is also used to relieve strain due to overwork.

This plant is a favorite with children, because if a leaf is picked and put in a book or a dark place, little plants sometimes grow from the notches in the margins of the leaves. Some believe that if little plants do grow, it is a sign that the one you love will soon become your sweetheart.

Other names: kalanchoe, leaf of life, love bush, travel life, calabana, sweetheart bush, temetic, wonder-of-world, kawakte lezom, lamowi.

Gliricidia

Gliricidia sepium

Gliricidia is native to South America and has been planted all over the tropics, but it does not naturalize readily. The reason you see it along many roadsides is that cuttings of considerable diameter can be stuck in the ground and they will root. Consequently it is commonly known and used as a living fence. The beautiful pink flowers bloom in the dry season when the trees are leafless.

Gliricidia fixes nitrogen and thrives on depleted soil. The leaves are used to feed sheep, cattle, goats and to cover meat being smoked. The seeds, bark, leaves and roots are all poisonous to mice and other rodents. The name is from *gliris* for dormouse and *caedo*, to kill. It is reported that the leaves are also poisonous to horses and dogs.

The wood is attractive, takes a good polish and can be used for furniture. It also resists termites and fungi. It is hard and used for fence posts and house supports.

A tea made with five leaves for children or ten leaves for adults is taken with sugar to cure coughs. Crushed leaves are put into a bath to treat skin infections. In Dominica, a scraped root or the leaves are used to treat gonorrhea.

Other names: mother-of-cocoa, quickstick, glory cedar, gloricidia.

Calabash

Crescentia cujete

A Caribbean native, the calabash can be distinguished at a glance by its clusters of leaves on long straight wand-like branches. The fruits are like gourds, from 4 to 12 inches in diameter. They are nearly round and turn from green to brown when ripe.

The flowers grow from the trunk or from the larger branches, not from the slender twigs. This is a necessary adaptation, as the heavy fruits would break the delicate branches. The flowers are a good source of nectar for honeybees.

The fruits have been used since Carib times for all kinds of containers. They make ideal bailers for fishermen, are handy bowls in the kitchen, useful as containers for carrying things and now they are carved and sold for souvenirs. The wood is very attractive and is used for small pieces, such as jewelry boxes.

Several parts of the calabash tree are used herbally. People who work in the bush sometimes rub the fruit pulp on their skin to protect themselves from any kind of skin poisoning. The pulp is also used for sprains and malignant tumors. Pulp from unripened fruits is boiled with the leaves and taken as a remedy for diabetes, and a syrup made from the cooked pulp is widely acclaimed as a cure for coughs and colds. The raw pulp is a purgative and is said to be poisonous to birds. Some obeah remedies require that concoctions be taken from a calabash bowl.

About the only disadvantage of the calabash tree is that it causes abortions in pregnant cattle if they eat any of the fallen fruits. All in all, the calabash has proved a very handy plant and it is not hard to see why the people of St. Lucia have chosen it as their national tree.

Other names: calebassier, calbas.

Tamarind

Tamarindus indica

Tamarind trees, very common along the roadside, come from India. The trees have dense dark green rounded crowns and are long lived. Brown lumpy pods, about three inches long, can usually be seen hanging from the tree. At the proper stage of ripeness, the pulp that surrounds the seeds has a tart but good flavor. Judging when the pod is right for eating is difficult for the uninitiated, but you can always ask local children. They are experts in this matter.

In the West Indies tamarind pulp is made into a refreshing drink and added to curries and preserves. It is used extensively in Indian cooking and is an ingredient in

Lea and Perrins Worcester sauce which may explain why that is so delicious. The over-ripe fruits can be used to polish copper and brass.

The trees in tamarind plantations must be widely spaced because each tree exudes a poisonous chemical from its roots which kills competing vegetation. The ground beneath the trees looks as though it has been swept with a broom. For this reason tamarinds are sometimes used in India as firebreaks. They are resistant to hurricanes and can withstand long dry periods. They do less well where the soil is always wet. Like other legumes, tamarinds fix nitrogen.

The hard and heavy wood is used to make furniture, boats and wheels. It is difficult to work but takes a good polish. The wood produces superior charcoal. Tamarind does not seem to be used much herbally in the Caribbean but it is used widely in African and Indian medicine.

Other names: tamarin, tamarinier, tamarin bord-de-mer, tanmawen.

Lantana
Lantana camara

Lantana is a woody shrub with opposite leaves which are coarsely textured and stems which are square in cross section. The fruits are dark blue berries. The name wild sage comes from the pleasant aroma of crushed leaves. This may also explain why the leaves are used to wash smelly ramgoats and why it is called ramgoat bush.

Several species of lantana are found in the West Indies and the most common, *Lantana camara,* probably originated here. Some species are named, but many lantanas don't fit neatly into a recognized category. *Lantana camara* flowers are yellow when they first open, but then they turn orange, and later, red. Other species have pink or pink and yellow flowers. Butterflies visit and pollinate the flowers. The seeds are dispersed by birds, as well as by humans, and the plant has spread to disturbed areas in the tropics world-wide. Lantanas remain bright and healthy even when they are mistreated. They are planted as annuals or houseplants in temperate zones.

The leaves are full of alkaloids and there are many accounts of lantana poisoning of cattle and sheep, which is one reason lantana is considered a pest in the tropics world-wide. But, except for domesticated animals, the plant is almost never eaten by herbivores.

It is used as a herbal remedy for diabetes and in the treatment of bruises, sprains and sores. A tea made from the leaves is used for colds, chills or yellow fever. For a skin rash on the head, the leaves are mixed with lard, cod liver oil and sulphur and the mixture is applied to the affected area twice a day.

Other names: wild sage, yellow sage, mille fleurs, sauge, ramgoat bush, bwa wa tout, pis-a-bed, jiwof fle, bwise.

Castor bean
Ricinus communis

Castor bean is probably a native of Africa, but it now grows around the world, even in temperate climates. It is a tall annual, often reaching the height of a small tree. It has escaped from cultivation and is often seen by the roadside and in waste places. The big star-shaped leaves of this weedy shrub are often tinged with red. The long leaf stalks are hollow and attached near the center of the leaves, so they form lopsided umbrellas. Male and female flowers are borne on the same plant, the males below the females. The big, shiny seeds develop within a three-sided capsule which is covered with weak prickles.

When pressed, the seeds yield castor oil, a poisonous, though useful, product. Ancient Egyptians used the oil in lamps. Until this century, its main use in the western world was in medicine, mainly as a purgative. Now only a small portion of the output is used in medicine and its usefulness in industry has greatly ex-

Sensitive plant

panded. Castor oil does not congeal at low temperatures, a desirable attribute. It is used in the manufacture of high grade lubricants, soaps, plastics, printing inks, in textile dyeing and for preserving leather. The hydrogenated oil is used in waxes, polishes, carbon paper, candles and crayons. It makes a protective coating for fabrics and is a constituent of hydraulic fluid. Because it produces a film which stays flexible and does not yellow with age, it is used in paints and varnishes. An insecticide is made from the leaves and the stems are used as a source of pulp and cellulose for making cardboard containers and newsprint. Not a bad record for a weed.

The seeds contain a toxic protein, ricin, which acts as a blood coagulant. It can cause nausea, muscle spasms and convulsions. Eating even a single seed can cause serious illness and more may be fatal. Despite this, it has been used in herbal medicine. Flu and headache are treated by applying a poultice from the leaves. Castor oil on cotton is used for earaches and an extract of the seeds has been used to treat colds, providing a cure that may be worse than the disease.

Other names: castor oil plant, carapate, ricin, gwen makwisti, pye gwen, palma Christi.

Woman's tongue
Albizia lebbek

As many of its names suggest, you may hear this plant before you see it -- which cannot be said of very many plants. The large straw-colored pods rattle noisily in the smallest breeze. The pods are often abundant and they contrast sharply with the dark wide-spreading foliage of this tree, introduced from tropical Asia. The leaves are composed of many small leaflets. The pods have a single row of seeds which look like thinly wrapped bumps, sort of a natural blister pack. The cream colored flowers are fragrant and are like tiny feather dusters. These trees are particularly common in dry areas and are well suited to poor soils because they can fix nitrogen. The leaves make excellent fodder. The wood was at one time exported from India to Europe under the name "East Indian walnut," and it is an excellent furniture wood.

Other names: mother-in-law's tongue, ladies tongue shack-shack, langua-a-via-femme, siris.

Annatto
Bixa orellana

Annatto is a pink-flowered shrub which grows to 15 feet high. The stems are densely hairy and rusty colored. The red seed pods are about two inches long and each contains from 30 to 50 heart-shaped seeds. It is grown around houses and occasionally escapes to the roadside. The bright red seeds were used by the Caribs and Central American Indians as body paint and as an insect repellent. It is reported to work especially well against mosquitos. It is not clear whether annatto was brought to the Caribbean islands by Amerindians or is a native species.

A tasteless orange or red dye is made by boiling the seeds in cooking oil. It was in use well before Columbus arrived. Now it is used as a food coloring for rice, butter, margarine, soups, and cheese. Annatto is also used herbally for diabetes.

Other names: roucou, roucoyer, rucu, roucu, woucou.

Lion's tail
Leonotis nepetifolia

Lion's tail is originally from Africa but is now found throughout the tropics. The single four-sided stem has bunches of flowers like pompoms. The orange flowers soon turn brown and you often see the curious looking stems with brown balls on them. They are used in decorations.

The leaves of lion's tail are the most

common ingredient of bush teas. These teas are used for fevers or as a bath for prickly heat. Other mixtures with lion's tail are used for worms, tuberculosis, pneumonia, stomach aches, hoarseness, coughs and cold. The leaves are sometimes crushed and the juice taken with a little salt instead of in a tea. It causes an allergic reaction in some people.

Other names: gwo-tet, Johnny Collins, bird honey, Lord Lavington, bald head, gros-bouton, grow pompom, gros tete, pompom soldat, man piabba, lion's ear.

Saman
Samanea saman

There is a story, popular in St. Lucia, about how this tree got one of its names. Some time ago a tourist asked the name of the wide spreading tree he was standing under. The answer came in patois: "massav," which means "I don't know." The tourist thought massav was the name of the tree and it has been called this ever since. Perhaps the tourist was in Columbus Square in Castries, St. Lucia, where there is a classic specimen.

The saman tree is more often called raintree and there are at least two very different versions of how this came about. Botanist Richard Howard says that it is because the leaflets move to a vertical position at night and collect moisture which is released when the leaves straighten in the morning. Daniel Janzen believes it is because the tree is favored by a sap-sucking bug. When hoards of these defecate, there is a steady drizzle beneath the tree. Massav.

These magnificent and enormous trees are native to Mexico and much of South America and are planted for shade and beauty. The trunk is short and stout and the tree is commonly at least twice as wide as it is high. The leaflets are almost diamond shaped and a large tree will have tens of thousands of pink powder puff flowers. Some of these develop into sweet seed pods which smell like liquorice and are relished by cattle.

The leaflets fold together in response to shade or cloud and in the folded position they contribute very little to the growth of the tree. It is no use trying to grow a saman in the shade of another tree, as it will amount to nothing.

Other names: raintree, massav, cocos tamarind, arbre a la pluie.

West Indian mahogany
Swietenia mahagoni

West Indian mahogany grows in both dry and humid forests. Forest trees have become scarce due to over-cutting, but mahogany trees have been planted in towns and along roads. They have big pear-shaped seed capsules which are held at the outside of the leaves and are quite noticeable. When the five sided capsules split open, the winged seeds are well positioned to be blown a long way from the parent tree.

The dark green leaves have from eight to ten leaflets which are unequally divided by the mid-vein. The bottom half of each leaflet is smaller than the top half. The introduced Honduran mahogany *(Swietenia macrophylla)* is similar to the native West Indian mahogany, but all parts are larger. West Indian mahogany leaves are from four to seven inches long. Honduran mahogany leaves are from eight to sixteen inches long.

A destructive insect attacks the new shoots of mahogany trees and has caused serious losses in plantations. A hybrid of the two mahoganies *(Swietenia aubrevilleana)* seems to be more resistant and is being tried in some reforestation efforts.

Mahogany seeds are packed with tannins to keep seed eaters away. If you don't mind having a lingering astringent taste in your mouth, try touching one to your tongue. Sections of the woody seed pods are used in craft work after they have split apart and released the seeds.

The beautiful wood of West Indian mahogany is considered superior to Honduran mahogany. Even the stumps of large trees are sometimes dug up because the uneven-grained wood is so highly prized.

Ginger Thomas
Tecoma stans

Ginger Thomas is native both to the West Indies and Central America. Poor soil, a dry climate and sea spray do not deter this little tree. Its prolific bright yellow flowers enliven the most barren environments and their sweet smell draws bees.

The long seed pods, too, are conspicuous, hanging like slender fingers, at first green and then brown when they mature. Each seed pod splits open, releasing the many small brown seeds with papery wings to the wind.

Other names: yellow elder, Christmas hope, coribee, bois caraibe, bois pissenlit, bois fleur jaunes, flambeaux.

Dumps
Ziziphus mauritiana

Children love to eat dumps, but to some of the rest of us they are quite tasteless. They are like small apples, green when young and orange to red when ripe.

You can recognize the tree by its roundness: round crown, round leaves and round apples. Not round are the two short spines at the base of each leaf. The twigs and the undersides of the leaves are covered with whitish or rust-colored hairs. Clusters of tiny flowers grow from the bases of the leaves.

Dumps are native to Asia and Africa. In the islands they frequently grow along roads, either planted or naturalized.

Other names: surette, pomme surrette, jujube, stink tree, dunk, apple dum.

Castor bean

Calabash

Common ground dove
Columbina passerina

The common ground dove is one of the smallest members of the pigeon family. It is just over six inches long, a little better than half the length of the next biggest commonly seen dove, the zenaida dove. Common ground doves are usually in small flocks on the ground and are very well camouflaged as they bob from side to side looking for grass seeds. They are colored and patterned much like bare ground. Sometimes they will eat berries and fruits. They are quite tame, but if you get too close they will fly off, showing their rufous wing patches. They nest on or near the ground, usually in spring or early summer.

Other names: ortolan, scaly-breasted dove.

Zenaida dove
Zenaida aurita

Zenaida doves are reddish brown birds, eleven to twelve inches long, with light brown heads. The sides of the neck are an iridescent purple-violet and the wings have prominent black spots. The tail feathers are tipped with white, but this can best be seen when the birds fly. Their pigeon-like mournful cooing is rather monotonous. They feed on the ground, mostly on seeds, occasionally on fruits. Zenaida doves will perch in trees when they are not feeding and they usually nest on the ground or in a low tree in a nest made of small twigs.

Like other members of the pigeon family, both parents produce a nutritious secretion of the crop which is fed to newly hatched birds.

Other names: turtle dove, mountain dove.

Glossy or shiny cowbird
Molothrus bonariensis

The male glossy cowbird is black with a violet gloss. The female is grayish-brown above, her wings and tail are dusky brown, and her underparts are light brownish grey. They superficially resemble carib grackles but the glossy cowbird has brown eyes and the carib grackle has bright yellow eyes. Glossy cowbirds are quite musical and their song is a mix of whistles and warbles.

Glossy cowbirds are recent arrivals from South America. Like North American cowbirds, they lay their eggs in the nests of other birds, an unpopular habit called brood parasitism. It is especially unpopular in the islands because glossy cowbirds tend to choose related species as foster parents, and among their relatives are the orioles. Martinique, St. Lucia and Montserrat each has a unique oriole species and the cowbird may already be having a negative effect on oriole populations, particularly in Martinique. They were first recorded in 1948 and are now very common. Glossy cowbirds are birds of open woodland and grassland, a habitat most common on Martinique.

Using other birds to sit on your eggs and raise your offspring seems like a winning strategy. Why don't more birds do it? Studies of female brown-headed cowbirds in North America reveal that these birds lay a whopping 40 eggs a year, of which only two or three survive to adulthood.

Gray kingbird, piperie
Tyrannus dominicensis

This very common bird can frequently be seen on telephone wires, moving its head back and forth like a radar scanner, searching for insects. It is a favorite with children and many of them know songs and poems about the pipirie. Pipirie is a rough approximation of the bird's call, which is noisily repeated throughout the day.

The gray kingbird is handsome: dark gray above and off-white on the belly and breast. A dark stripe goes back from the base of the long heavy bill back across the eye. The tail is forked.

Gray kingbirds dart out for flying insects and usually snap them up in mid air. Sometimes insects are plucked from vegetation. If insects are in short supply, fruits, including the berries from gumbo limbo and royal palm, are substituted.

In spring and early summer gray kingbirds build flimsy stick nests which they line with grasses. The female incubates the eggs and both parents feed the little ones.

ANIMALS

Mongoose
Herpestes auropunctatus

The mongoose is probably the most commonly seen wild mammal on most islands. They are very speedy animals, often seen as a brown blur with a bushy tail crossing the road and disappearing into the bush without a trace. The mongoose is a controversial creature: a very appealing, intelligent animal that has had a devastating effect on many reptiles and birds. Young mongooses make wonderful pets, but no matter how hard you try to control an adult, it will sooner or later begin decimating the local chicken and wild bird population. In addition, on islands where rabies exists, they are major carriers.

The mongoose was first introduced to Jamaica by M. Espeut in 1872 to kill rats that were destroying sugar cane. There the mongoose was called Mr. Espeut's Rat.

People also hoped they would get rid of all the snakes. Rudyard Kipling's Rikki Tikki Tavi story led people to think that mongooses live on snakes, but probably they are never a large part of the mongoose diet. They like a varied diet of birds, birds' eggs, rodents, insects and some fruit, especially paw paw. Sugar cane growers were disappointed in the mongoose. It feeds by day and doesn't climb trees. Rodents spent their nights eating sugar cane and could climb trees to escape the mongoose if necessary.

Mongooses grow to be about 16 inches long, with an additional ten inches in tail. Their reputation for ferocity is well deserved. They are highly agile animals and can run up to a wall at full speed and then turn the corner without slowing down. They run in leaps. Mongoose parents stay together and both raise the young.

Dominica has no mongooses, but they are established on most other large islands. Lizards have probably suffered the most from the mongoose, but they also kill snakes, ground-nesting birds, destroy turtle eggs, and have been implicated in the demise of the agouti in Grenada. Both ground and tree-nesting birds have to watch out for another mammal, the manicou (opossum), as well, for manicous have similar appetites and are good at climbing trees.

©Kati Shea

Plants
1. Avocado
2. Soursop
3. Passion fruit
4. Grapefruit
5. Sugar apple
6. Banana
7. Paw paw
8. Cocoa
9. Pineapple
10. Dasheen
11. Screw pine
12. Breadfruit

Birds
13. Broadwing hawk
14. Yellow warbler
15. Cattle egret

Animals
16. Giant toad

Agriculture is the major industry in many Caribbean islands, but life is not easy for the farmer. The flatter islands are seasonally dry and the mountainous islands are -- mountainous. Competition from producers in Central America and Africa is keen and they often have far larger fields and a more equable climate. All tropical crops are at peril from fungi and bacteria, organisms that thrive in moist heat, and pesticides are needed here more than in temperate zones. Farmers in the islands are too small a group to do effective marketing, export markets are far away and much of the produce is highly perishable. Even simple things, like finding a reliable source of seeds which are adapted to Caribbean conditions, can be a challenge. Most farming is done in valleys and lowlands, on soil that has eroded from the higher mountains.

The first farmers were the pre-Columbian Arawak inhabitants who brought plants and animals with them when they migrated from South America. It is believed they bought agoutis (an edible rodent) for meat, and plants such as pineapples and annatto. When Europeans came to the islands, they discovered that they could grow many new crops, and they established profitable small farms. All this changed with the arrival of sugar, when the small farms gave way to large plantations based on slave labor.

Now farming varies from island to island. In some islands most of the land remains in the hands of a few plantation owners. In others, more equal land distribution means that small farmers choose their own crops. When families own land they tend to grow fruit trees and plants that provide much of their own food, and any surplus is sold at the market. In the past few years, important crops like bananas and cocoa have fallen on hard times. There is a trend to export more specialty fruits such as mangos and soursop, though currently this is on a small scale.

Sugar cane
Saccharus officinarum

Sugar cane is a member of the grass family, but you would have trouble mowing it, as it grows twelve feet high. Its wild ancestor originated in eastern Asia. Unlike most grasses, its woody stems are filled with a sweet sap. The production of sugar by boiling the juice was first discovered in India, probably in the first millennium BC.

Sugar cane was so important to the history of the Caribbean between 1650 and 1850 that one historian wrote: "The history of this period is in fact the history of sugar." Most of the trade between Europe and this region consisted of slaves coming in and sugar, rum and molasses going back. Sugar sold for an extremely high price and, even as late as 1744, the value of the crops in the West Indies was greater than those of all the North American colonies. The first sugar mill was set up in Barbados in 1640 and by 1651 there were 20,000 slaves on that island.

In the early days of sugar, each estate had its own sugar mill. These were powered by cattle, the wind, or by water, and the crumbling remains of windmills can be seen on many islands. Later, processing was centralized and a few tall chimneys of those sugar factories still stand. Sugar and rum factories still operate, and a handful are powered by water wheels.

Sugar cane is a heavy feeder and the soil is impoverished further because very little organic matter is returned. Instead the dry stalks, or begasse, is fed to animals or used to fuel the fires beneath the giant cauldrons in which the sap is boiled.

In the heyday of sugar production vast areas of forest were cleared to plant sugar cane, and much more forest -- on land that

Rich agricultural land in Mespotamia Valley, St. Vincent, including fields of bananas

Cattle egret in sugar cane, St. Kitts

was too steep to till -- was cut to provide wood to add to the fires beneath the cauldrons. This reckless passion for profit caused a great increase in the number of people held in slavery and forever changed the landscape of the islands.

The beginning of the end came when sugar was extracted from the sugar beet in Austria in 1797. Slavery was abolished in the British territories in 1834 and by 1883 the volume of beet sugar surpassed cane sugar for the first time. Now much of the machinery is run by electricity and the begasse is used to make particle board.

Rum is a sugar cane product. It was first produced in the Caribbean in the early sixteenth century and is still an important source of income on many islands. On the English islands, rum is produced by the fermentation of molasses by yeast. The alcoholic soup that results is then distilled. On French islands, cane juice is fermented directly, without conversion to molasses. This rum (or rhum) has a much stronger flavor.

A lot of sugar cane is still grown on St. Kitts and Barbados, and pockets can be seen on other islands, mainly in the drier areas. A cane field is established by planting cuttings or setts, which are short pieces of the jointed stem, each containing a bud.

The plants are full grown in a year and are then cut close to the ground. New shoots grow from the roots and the field can go on indefinitely. For best yields, however, the fields must be replanted every seven to eight years.

Bananas and plantains
Musa species

There are two main groups of bananas. The eating banana that is sold in northern supermarkets originated in the Malay archipelago. The other kind of banana (often called a plantain) that is used for cooking, originated in southern India. They are both plants of the humid lowland Old World tropics. In tropical America their ecological niche is occupied by the closely related heliconias (balisiers). Bananas require a lot of light and fertile soils, as they are shallow rooted. Often they need to be staked against the wind. Nowadays there are many varieties of bananas used for eating or cooking and many hybrids. Most eating bananas grow with their fingers pointing up and most cooking bananas grow with their fingers pointing down.

About half the world's banana crop is eaten raw when ripe and the other half is eaten as a cooked vegetable. Plantains are a staple food in much of Africa, India and tropical America, but they haven't caught on in the far east.

Bananas were brought to the Caribbean from the Canary Islands in 1516 by a Spanish priest and they have been here ever since. They are a major crop in the mountainous islands from Dominica to Grenada. For years the English-speaking Windwards have had a contract to sell bananas to the shipper Geest. Almost all of the crop has gone to the United Kingdom, under a favorable trade agreement. Banana growers now face an uncertain future as the prospect of a united Europe approaches. In Central and South America, where land is flatter and easier to farm, banana yields are as high as 16-20 tons per acre compared to an average of only 10 tons per acre in the Windwards. As the realities of free trade unfold, yields and quality must both improve if the industry is to survive.

You may see bananaquits, hummingbirds, bees and many other large insects on the flowers, but several features suggest that bats were once the primary pollinators, back before people took on the job of banana reproduction. Banana flowers produce abundant nectar and sticky pollen, the kind of sizeable reward that bats need to make their visits worthwhile. The flowers open at night and have the fetid odor that bats fancy. The flowers are big and strong enough to hold a fat little mammal, and the flower parts are dull in color. People propagate bananas by planting pieces of the underground stem, but they can be coaxed into setting seed, a necessity when new varieties are sought.

After a piece of the underground stem is planted, it takes about nine months to get bananas. Though they are often called trees because of their large size, the banana doesn't even have a true stem until the flower stalk emerges. Each leaf begins at the base of the plant; the "stem" consists of tightly wrapped leaf bases. The single-stemmed flower shoot forces its way through the center of the rolled up leaf bases. It emerges out the top and soon bends toward the ground under the weight of the heavy flower. Big red bracts unfold from the flower bud, and under each bract is a layer of flowers. These will soon become a hand of bananas. A bunch contains from five to twenty hands, and each hand has from two to twenty fruits.

The big towering plant dies after it has fruited. The old plant is cut down and sometimes the leaves are used to make mats and baskets. One of the new suckers (shoots) that springs up from the base of the mother plant is left to produce the next crop. To ensure good yields, the whole field is replanted every four to six years, but a banana plant is potentially immortal and fields nearly a hundred years old are known.

When you look at a field of bananas you may see blue bags covering the fruits. These are to prevent the bananas getting scratched when they are small. A climbing bird or a even a banana leaf brushing against the bananas will leave marks. They do no real harm to the banana, but they do hurt the grower, for he or she can't sell them.

You may hear bananas called "figs" in the West Indies. Bananas were known to the Arabs in ancient time and appear in the Koran as the "tree of paradise" which is similar enough to the Christian "tree of knowledge" that the fruits got mixed up. They were called figs in Europe in the tenth century. Though the name has been lost in Europe and North America, it survives in the islands.

Cocoa, cacao, cocoa tree
Theobroma cacao

Theobroma means "food for the gods." Cocoa and chocolate are made from the seeds of the cacao or cocoa tree. This small tree is often laden with orange or pink hanging pods. Cocoa is an important crop in Grenada, but in most other islands the trees will be seen more often in small gardens or by the roadside.

The natural habitat of cocoa is in the deep shade of the lower story of the New World tropical rainforest. It grows only where the temperature is always above 60° F. The new leaves of the cocoa tree are red and often the leaves hang down to avoid the direct rays of the sun. Indeed, the leaves have two special joints, at either end of the leaf stem, and in dim light these are inflated and the leaf rises to catch the light. If the sunlight becomes too intense, the leaves are lowered and hang limply and do not intercept much sunlight.

In nature cocoa beans are distributed by monkeys and squirrels which chew through the pod to eat the sweet white pulp that surrounds the seeds in the seed pod. The bitter seeds are then tossed aside unharmed.

What happens to a seed that even monkeys and squirrels spit out to turn it into a substance that most humans love and many desperately crave? The answer is, a lot. People have been working with this bean for a long time.

Cocoa has been cultivated by the Indian cultures of Mexico for over 2000 years. When Spaniards arrived in the 16th century, they found that the Mayans, who lived in the wet lowlands, used beans as money. A slave is said to have been worth 100 beans. The Aztecs, living in a drier climate, were not able to cultivate this money-that-grows-on-trees, but they bought cocoa beans from the Mayans and made a drink called xocoatl by grinding the beans with red pepper, vanilla and water. Cocoa beans were brought to Europe by Columbus, but the Spaniards quickly jettisoned the red pepper and replaced it with sugar. In the 500 years since that first shipment, defatting, roasting and fermenting were discovered -- all part of what it takes to make what we call chocolate.

Nowadays, the seeds with the pulp that surrounds them are first put into sweat boxes to ferment. They need to be stirred often while they are fermenting, both to keep the temperature uniform and to keep them aerated. During this process chemical changes occur and the characteristic flavor and aroma of cocoa develop. After seven or eight days the seeds are spread out to dry. During the drying process they are 'danced' -- people in bare feet walk over the beans and shuffle them around so that they get a good polish. Some of the fat, or cocoa butter, is then squeezed out in a press, leaving the powder called cocoa. Sugar and some of the cocoa butter is then mixed with the whole ground-up beans to produce chocolate. Chocolate has more cocoa butter, and cocoa has less, than the original proportion in the bean.

Cocoa is a demanding crop. In addition to shade, protection from drying winds is important. Like cocoa, fungi love humidity, so diseases are an ever-present threat. A mature tree will develop about 10,000 flowers every year. A curious feature is that groups of flowers grow directly from the bark of the main stem or large branches. Only from 10 to 50 of these develop into pods, but they are big and heavy. If they grew from slender branches like most fruits, the weight would break them. There are basically three cocoa types. Criollo, with red to orange pods, has been in cultivation since ancient times. Forastero, whose pods are yellow, is from a different part of South America and has been grown for only the past 200 years. Trinitario is of even more recent origin and is a hybrid of the other two.

The cocoa tree is not related to the South American coca tree (*Erythroxylon coca*) from which cocaine is produced.

Avocado pear
Persea americana

Avocado trees can be seen in gardens and on farms. Like cocoa, the new leaves are reddish, turning green as they mature. The delicious fruits have more protein than any other fruit and an oil content varying from 5 to 25%. They are fairly rich in minerals and vitamins, particularly of the B complex, and vitamins A and E. The bad news is that they are packed with calories. However, the good news for winter visitors is

Cocoa trees with pods

that this won't be a problem, as the largest part of the crop matures in the summer, leaving just a few to ripen in the winter and spring.

Avocado trees usually grow about 30 feet tall. The species originated in Central America and early Spanish explorers found it in cultivation from Mexico to Peru. It was introduced to Jamaica in about 1650 and to other islands in the West Indies soon after.

Long ago, Darwin wrote that "Nature tells us in the most emphatic manner that she abhors perpetual self-fertilization." The avocado is one of many plants that appears to have been designed to show that he was on to something. This tree has developed an effective system for ensuring cross-fertilization. Avocado flowers contain both the male and female parts. But to make sure they don't fertilize themselves, they open twice. The first time the female parts are receptive, but no pollen is shed. They then close for from 12 to 36 hours. When they open again, pollen is shed, but the female part, the stigma, is no longer receptive. The sweet smelling flowers se-

crete nectar which is sought by bees, and once the flowering season gets going, the bees ensure plenty of cross pollination as they move from tree to tree.

The seed of the avocado is used medicinally. A paste of grated seed, mixed with clay and vinegar, is applied to pulled muscles or swollen glands.

Breadfruit
Artocarpus altilis

In 1793 Captain Bligh bought twelve hundred breadfruit trees from Tahiti to Jamaica and St. Vincent in the ship Providence. It was described as a "floating forest" when the ship sailed into the harbor in Jamaica. The breadfruit tree was directly responsible for the mutiny against Bligh in 1789, when he attempted to bring almost as many trees on the Bounty. The trees were in soil-filled casks and had to be carried below for warmth at night and brought out into the sun each day: an exhausting job for the overworked crew. The trees required copi-

Field of dasheen. The young leaves are used in calaloo soup.

ous waterings, which left the crew on short rations. When Bligh was set adrift, the trees were thrown overboard.

Breadfruit trees were brought to the Caribbean to provide cheap food for slaves, but the slaves didn't like them any more than Bligh's crew did. They preferred plantains. Breadfruit is rather tasteless if it is just boiled, but it is very good fried or baked. Breadfruit is a good source of carbohydrates, but lacks protein.

The breadfruit is at home in humid tropical lowlands. It is probably native to the Malay archipelago and traveled with humans to the Polynesian islands. There it is a very important food and is treated with the same reverence that Indians have for the mango. In addition to its usefulness as cheap food, the sticky, milky sap of breadfruit hardens when exposed to air and makes a glue or, when mixed with cotton, makes a caulking compound for boats. The dark green leaves make excellent cattle fodder.

In the Caribbean there are breadfruit trees wherever there are people. You will find this handsome tree very easy to identify. The shiny dark green leaves are big, from one to two feet long, and are deeply lobed.

The breadfruit tree is a freak of nature that would have died out had it not caught man's attention. For it produces no seeds with which to reproduce itself. Oddly, for a seedless tree where no fertilization takes place, the flowers still need to be pollinated or the fruits will not develop. The round fruits weigh up to ten pounds. New trees are made from pieces of root which are induced to sprout -- a process which requires some care.

Breadnut, a seeded form of the breadfruit, does produce seeds and they are good to eat when roasted. Jackfruit *(Artocarpus heterophyllus)*, a close relative, is occasionally seen. It, too, has big edible seeds. Breadfruits are easily injured and the climb-pick-throw-catch method is used for harvesting in St. Vincent and Dominica.

Bligh introduced several other plants to the Windwards and Leewards, including the ackee *(Blighia sapida)* from Jamaica.

Pigeon peas
Cajanus indicus

Almost anyone who grows vegetables in the islands will include a few pigeon peas in the garden. These perennial bushes can withstand drought, as they have a long taproot. They bear continually, and they can be eaten as fresh green peas or as dried peas. They fix nitrogen and so improve the soil. In addition, they are useful for erosion control and make good fodder for animals. They are even used in herbal medicine to treat white blood cell diseases. This probably explains why they are cultivated throughout the tropics, especially in dry areas.

Pigeon peas are probably native to Africa, where they are sometimes found growing wild. Seeds have been found in Egyptian tombs of the XIIth dynasty and they were cultivated there before 2000 BC. By this time the Egyptians were trading with tropical Africa.

You may notice two varieties. Both grow about four feet high. On one kind the flowers are all yellow and on the other they are streaked with red.

Dasheen, eddo, tannia

These three very similar plants, along with yams and potatoes, are called "ground provisions" in the islands. They are grown in the wetter hilly districts and are brought to town to be sold at the market. You would have trouble finding a more confusing group of plants. Not only are there many common names, but botanists don't agree on their Latin names. Together they form a major food crop, not just in the West Indies, but world-wide in the tropics.

They all are in the aroid family, which is also home to such plants as jack-in-the-pulpits and anthuriums. The leaves grow out of the ground and are usually spear-shaped, with one point at the tip and two others pointing backwards. The strange phallic flower stalk, with many tiny flowers, is this family's hallmark.

They may be one of the oldest cultivated crops on earth. Archaeologists have unearthed ancient irrigated terrace systems which they believe were used for edible aroids before rice was known. It may be that rice first came to man's notice as a weed in the dasheen patch. As well as having an ancient past, the edible aroids may have a promising future. Dasheen starch has particles only one tenth the size of those in corn starch and can be used for pharmaceutical grade powders or added to biodegradable plastics to improve breakdown.

The first attempts to eat these vegetables must have been very unpleasant because the tubers of all aroids contain calcium oxalate crystals which are broken down only when the root is thoroughly cooked. Eating raw dasheen is like eating a potato packed with fiberglass. Calcium oxalate is in the leaves as well as the roots and undoubtedly discourages other predators that haven't learned to boil their food.

There are infinite varieties of dasheen, eddo and tannia around the world and, contrary to the usual rules, they have all come about through vegetative reproduction (non-sexual propagation, without the benefit of gene mixing). A given plant may not have the same number of chromosomes in each cell: some cells have as few as 22 and others as many as 42. From time to time interesting mutations crop up and growers, over thousands of years, have propagated some of those that seemed to be better than usual.

DASHEEN (*Colocasia esculenta* var. *esculenta*) grows to three feet high. One of the most popular varieties (cultivars) in the West Indies has a large purple spot on the leaf. Dasheen has a large central corm or bulb and a few much smaller side tubers or cormels. **EDDO** (*Colocasia esculenta* var. *antiquorum*) has a smaller central corm and more, larger cormlets. Both eddo and dasheen are called taro in the Pacific and make a good substitute for potatoes. When cooked, they are similar in food value to potatoes, but have somewhat more protein.

Eddos are thought to have developed in China and Japan from dasheen. They can be grown where there is less rainfall than is required for dasheen.

Calaloo soup is made from the young leaves of either eddo or dasheen, although sometimes vine spinach, an inferior substitute, is used.

TANNIA (*Xanthosoma sagittifolium*) is native to the Caribbean and was cultivated here before Columbus' visit. It is more robust and disease-resistant than dasheen or eddo and tolerates even more dryness than eddo. The leaves grow up to six feet high, about twice as big as dasheen, and the roots are more gnarled and hairy. Dasheen and eddo are more cylindrical. Tannia can be boiled, baked, or parboiled and then fried. In Dominica mashed tannia is mixed with coconut, sugar, spices and eggs and baked as a pudding.

Guava
Psidium guajava

You will see guava jelly and guava cheese in many shops, and the guava shrub is almost as easy to find. You can identify it by its peeling brown bark which reveals a green stem surface. The bark is used as a remedy for worms. The fruits are cultivated and naturalized throughout the West Indies. Birds, too, love the fruits and widely distribute the seeds, suitably fertilized. This crooked branchy shrub grows along roadsides, in gardens and in the dry bush. The simple elliptic leaves have prominent veins and the five-petalled flowers have a dense brush of stamens. The nice smelling pulp of the fruit can be yellow, pink or red.

Guavas contain a large amount of vitamin A and several times the amount of vitamin C found in citrus fruits. Guava cheese is not cheese. It is a paste made by evaporating guava pulp after mixing it with sugar.

Guava

Mango

Mangifera indica

The mango has been described as "a ball of tow (string) soaked in turpentine and molasses, and you have to eat it in the bath tub." It has also been described as the most delicious fruit in the world. There are thousands of varieties, and the range in quality of fruit is immense. Fruits from seedlings can be stringy, watery and taste like turpentine and they couldn't be more different from the fruits from the best varieties.

Some mangos are exported, though they don't ship very well. Their real economic importance is in local consumption in every village in the Caribbean.

Mangos may come from India, as the Latin name suggests, but this is not clear. They have been cultivated in India for over 4000 years and their true origin may be Burma or Malaya. Mangos are the most popular fruit among millions of people in the Orient, particularly in India, where it takes the place the apple has in temperate zones. Mangos were introduced to Brazil in the late 1600's, and were brought from Brazil to Barbados in 1742.

You will see mango trees just about everywhere, though they are most productive in areas that have a pronounced dry season, as they depend on pollinating insects. These insects are much more active when they aren't getting pelted by raindrops (just as you or I would choose to lay low if thousands of enormous boulders were falling from the sky).

Mangos have very deep taproots, from 18 to 25 feet long, which help them get through a sustained dry spell. The trees have very dense, rounded, dark green crowns and grow to 60 feet high. The

118

Screw pine growing by the roadside; note the prop roots.

leaves come out in flushes and the new leaves are first reddish, then pale green, and finally dark green. They are long and thin and smell like turpentine when crushed. A milky latex flows from cut twigs.

Mango trees produce a dense shade. The ripe fruits have nearly as much vitamin A as butter and can be eaten raw or made into juices, jams, or preserves. Unripe fruits are made into pickles and chutneys. Many trees do not bear fruit every year. Julie, a popular variety in the islands, does bear reliably, but is slow growing. The delicious cultivars must be propagated by grafting.

Mango trees produce a good quality timber which is used for many things, including boatbuilding.

Nutmeg
Myristica fragrans

Not long ago Grenada produced 25% of the world's supply of nutmegs, but recently the industry fell on hard times when a trade agreement with Indonesia was broken. Nutmegs were introduced to Grenada in 1843 from the Moluccas, but were not planted commercially until around 1860. In the early 1900's there was a large increase in production and nutmegs became Grenada's most important export. In 1955 Hurricane Janet destroyed an estimated 80% of the trees. In the ensuing years there has been considerable replanting. The occasional nutmeg tree can also be found on other mountainous islands.

Nutmegs thrive where there is no pronounced dry season, which is usually at higher elevations. The oval, smooth-edged leaves are dark green on the upper surface, but much lighter below. The fruits are the shape, size and color of a large apricot. There are three layers which surround the nutmeg proper and each is used for a different purpose. The outer part of the 'apricot' is called the pericarp or husk, and is used to make nutmeg jelly. It splits open on one side while still on the tree,

revealing the lustrous seed inside. The seed is wrapped in a lacy brilliant red covering. When dried and ground to a powder, this covering becomes the spice mace, which is used extensively in the preparation of sauces and ketchups. Next comes a dark outer shell which has to be removed before using the nutmeg inside. This layer is used as a flower bed mulch. Both nutmeg and mace contain myristicin, a narcotic which keeps the nut from being eaten by some predators and which is poisonous to humans in large doses.

The nutmeg poses a problem to the farmer. The male and female flowers are borne on different trees and there is no easy way to tell them apart until they flower at about five years of age. At this point, most of the male trees are pulled up and tossed, for one male can pollinate ten of the nutmeg-bearing female trees.

Screw pine, common screw pine
Pandanus utilis

The screw pine would definitely be a screwy pine, if it were a pine, but it is not. It is a flowering plant in the family Pandan-aceae. Like palms, the trunks of these primitive plants do not get much thicker after they have formed. Unlike palms, they commonly branch. They have straight prop roots, though on some trees you may have to lift up the hanging leaves to see them. When the leaves are shed, an impression is left on the trunk which looks like the threads of a screw. The fruit looks a little like a topless pineapple. Hence the name screw pine.

The edges of the long leaves are formidably barbed all along their length and even the underside of the midrib of the leaf has curved spines. The long leaf cannot support itself and buckles, folding about half to two thirds of the way from the base. Water is carried away from the folded part so it cannot stay on the leaf surface and leach nutrients. It runs down to the encircling leaf bases where a mound of vegetable and animal debris collects. The screw pine may be able to collect nutrients from this water, as some bromeliads do.

Screwpines are from the old world tropics but were introduced to the Caribbean in the 1700's and are used extensively both for local use and in the handicrafts industry. They make good thatch and can be woven into beautiful baskets. Before they are used for weaving, the marginal prickles are removed and then the leaf is cut in two to remove the central prickles. The long flexible pieces are up to six feet long. If air dried, screw pine is brown, but if dried in an oven it stays a creamy white. By using both drying methods, patterns can be made in mats and baskets. The fruit is in segments and can be taken apart. When dried, each part makes a small short-handled brush. Good brushes can also be made by beating the ends of pieces of the prop roots.

Pawpaw, papaya
Carica papaya

Almost every garden has a pawpaw tree. Pawpaws are fast growing and the juicy big melon-like fruits can be harvested within a year of planting a seed. The trees go on producing for years, but they tend to grow so tall after two or three years that it is hard to pick the fruits. The soft-wooded hollow stem is usually unbranched and only the upper leaves stay on, leaving an umbrella-shaped tree. The big, deeply lobed leaves are on long petioles (leaf stalks) and when they die and fall off, they leave noticeable marks on the trunk.

Male and female flowers are usually on different plants and in commercial planting six seeds are planted for each tree. When they flower and reveal their gender, most of the males are weeded out. Male flowers are borne on long stalks. The female flowers and the fruits are on short stalks, clustered below the leaves.

Pawpaws don't travel well, so most are eaten locally. They are eaten fresh or used for drinks, jams, or ice cream. They are rich in vitamins A and C.

The leaves, fruits and milky latex sap all contain the enzyme papain, which is used as a meat tenderizer because it digests protein. Meat can be wrapped in papaya leaves or boiled with the leaves to tenderize it, but don't leave it too long or the meat will turn to shreds. Papain is also used to clarify beer, in chewing gum, in cosmetics, in the tanning industry for bathing hides, for degumming natural silk, to give shrink resistance to wool, and as a constituent of washing powders for laundry and dry cleaning. Papain is obtained by making vertical cuts in the unripe fruits and then collecting the milky latex.

The hollow petioles have been used as molds for making candles. Tea brewed from the boiled root is used as a herbal medicine to treat gonorrhea. Pawpaw seeds are eaten to rid the body of worms and a tea made from cubes of green pawpaw is said to be good for high blood pressure. Green pawpaw can also be cooked and used as a vegetable.

Pineapple, pine
Ananas comosus

The pineapple is in the bromeliad family. Most of its relatives are the epiphytes or air plants that you see perched on tree limbs or sometimes even on power lines.

They were widely cultivated in pre-Columbian times in South America and jars shaped liked pineapples have been found in pre-Inca graves. Columbus found pineapples growing in Guadeloupe in 1493 and reported to Ferdinand and Isabella that he had found fruits "resembling pine cones, very sweet and delicious." The Indians called the pineapple "ananas," meaning "fruit of excellence."

It is likely that pineapples were brought to the Caribbean by Amerindians. The fruit is smaller than the Hawaiian kind, but the flavor is considered superior. They taste so good when allowed to ripen on the plant that, if you taste one, you will probably eat the whole thing.

A single pineapple is the product of about 100 compacted flowers. Cuttings from the fruit tops or from side shoots are used to begin new plantings. Pineapples are shallow rooted and occasionally topple over. Sometimes they are planted closely so that the plants will prop each other up.

Bromeliads are among the few plants whose flowering can be manipulated by chemicals. Growers accidentally discovered that wood smoke caused mature plants to flower. It was later discovered that auto exhaust and even smog also work. Now big commercial growers rely on a synthetic organic chemical called "Omaflora" to induce flowering. If you have a bromeliad as a house plant and want it to flower, try enclosing it with a ripe apple for several days in a plastic bag, for ethylene, too, makes bromeliads flower. In nature, hummingbirds are the principal pollinating agents.

Soursop, sugar apple and their relatives

There are four common small fruit trees, all in the genus *Annona* and similar in appearance -- except for the fruits -- which grow wild and in gardens in the islands. All of the *Annonas* have six to 12 pairs of noticeable veins on the leaves. The leaves are easy to recognize. They are simple long ovals, pointed at both ends. They grow alternately along the branch in a very even fashion. All are native to the Lesser Antilles and all except the pond apple *(Annona glabra)* can withstand drought.

The soursop *(Annona muricata)* and the sugar apple or sweet sop *(Annona squamosa)* are the most common. Both are planted for their edible fruits, but they also grow wild in hedgerows. Soursop fruits are the only spiny ones. They are delicious

eaten fresh or when used for making drinks, ice cream or preserves. Left to themselves, soursops are not very productive. Serious growers hand-pollinate the blossoms and the yield of fruit increases markedly.

The sugar apple has a much smaller fruit but it is also very popular. The fruit is made of fleshy pads which can be pulled off and eaten and the soft pulp is very much like applesauce. They, too, are eaten fresh or made into drinks or sherbet. Custard apple or bullock's heart *(Annona reticulata)* fruits are roundish or heart shaped, with a clearly visible pattern on the surface. The pond apple is not used much. It grows in wet areas and has a smooth skin.

Passion fruit, maracudja, granadina
Passiflora edulis

Passion fruits are not normally grown on a large scale in the islands, but frequently a farmer will grow a vine or two and take the round yellow fruits to market. The climbing, woody vines can grow to be 50 feet long. The vines climb vigorously and can live for from three to ten years, clinging to a support with spiraling tendrils. The leaves are deeply three-lobed and early Spanish explorers thought the showy complex flowers symbolized the crucifixion. Passion fruits can be eaten by scooping out the flesh, but there are many small seeds mixed in and most people prefer the seedless juice. It is good in sherbets and fruit salads, too.

Citrus trees
Citrus species

Columbus brought the first citrus trees to the Caribbean on his second voyage. Citrus species originated in Asia but were common in Europe by the time Columbus set off. Oranges *(Citrus sinensis)*, limes *(Citrus aurantifolia)*, sour, sev-

Pineapples

ille or gospo oranges *(Citrus aurantium)*, and Mandarin oranges *(Citrus reticulata)* are all commonly grown. The Caribbean put its own stamp on citrus farming with the grapefruit *(Citrus paradisi)* which was developed in Barbados. It was first described in 1750 as the forbidden fruit of Barbados, though the name grapefruit came from Jamaica in 1830. You will find citrus trees in many gardens and in small plantations. They are eaten locally and used in the production of juices and drinks.

Some form of citrus is available year round and many are abundant right through the winter till May. Island oranges are often ready to eat when green. It is hard to assess the quality of oranges and grapefruits from viewing them, so it is advisable to taste a sample before buying a whole bag. Citrus trees can tolerate moderately dry conditions and limes manage to grow on some smaller, drier islands. If you crush a leaf of a citrus tree, it smells like the fruit. When cultivating citrus trees, it is usual to use a rootstock from the sour orange or lime, because these are more resistant to root rot. The desired sp⌐cies is then grafted onto the rootstock.

BIRDS

Cattle egret
Bubulcus ibis

Look for a cattle egret wherever you see a cow. These small white herons snap up lizards, as well as grasshoppers and other insects which show themselves as they move to escape being munched up or stepped on by cattle.

These are the smallest white herons, standing only 19 to 21 inches tall. They nest and roost in colonies, and will often fly between their roosting and feeding grounds in flocks. As they land in the evening, you can hear their rough croaking barks as they argue over the best branches on what is often a very crowded roosting tree. Both the colonies and roosts are usually near water.

The male defends the part of the branch that he has in mind for a nest and when his claim to the branch is established, both sexes begin to build. Twig theft is so common that when the male goes off for new material, the female incorporates the previous shipment into the nest and stands guard. The eggs are laid and hatch at two day intervals, so there are several sizes of chick in the nest. The youngest and smallest do not survive in years when food is scarce.

Cattle egrets are from Africa and were first reported in the Caribbean in 1933. No one knows how they made it over the Atlantic, but a hurricane may have helped. The second report came in 1944 and today they are the most common herons in the Caribbean and inhabit more than 50 good-sized islands. Their success in this expanded range has coincided with a big increase in the areas where cattle are grazed. They are completely at home with cattle and if you keep a sharp lookout, you may even see one sitting on a cow's back. Cattle egrets have a good source of food which few other birds use and they are the only species of heron able to breed in their first year.

Other names: white gaulin, cattle gaulin.

Yellow Warbler
Dendroica petechia

Yellow warblers are common in all lowland habitats and will follow agriculture up into the hills. Farmers should welcome these friends, for they are mostly insectivorous, gleaning insects from the bark, leaves and twigs of trees and shrubs. On occasion they snap up insects in the air and they can hover for a moment or engage in brief aerial pursuit.

The yellow warbler is the only bird that looks all yellow from a distance and it is the only warbler that nests in most of the islands. Yellow warblers have a large geographic range, from barren ground in far

124

northern Canada all the way to Mexico -- and from the Atlantic to the Pacific. Some yellow warblers live year-round on the islands and do not migrate. This population nests as far south as St. Lucia. Other yellow warblers that nest in North America come to the islands for the winter. Some from this group travel all the way to Grenada.

Each yellow warbler pair will defend a territory against other yellow warblers, even when they are not nesting. The nest, a compact cup of fibers and fine grasses with a lining of plant down and hair, is usually placed in the fork of a tree or shrub.

Unlike most birds, yellow warblers can recognize the eggs of a glossy cowbird in its nest. Glossy cowbirds are shady characters which get other birds to incubate their eggs and raise their young. The warblers are unable to remove the cowbird egg because it is too big. Instead, they consign it to the basement by building a new nest on top.

Broadwing hawk, malfini, chicken hawk
Buteo platypterus

Broadwings are the most common hawks in these islands, often seen soaring effortlessly, high above field and forest. The species name, *platypterus*, means broad wing, which fits. It is brown above and paler, irregularly barred or spotted with reddish brown, below. Bold tail bands of brown and white are of equal width. You may hear its call, a petulant high-pitched thin squeal, which sounds as though it is made by a very small bird.

When not circling, broadwings will perch, often for a long time, on an exposed branch. Their diet is an appetizing medley of snakes, lizards, frogs, small birds and rodents. Broadwing hawks nest in the spring and two to three eggs are laid in a bulky nest of twigs, high in a tree. Both parents take care of the eggs and the young birds.

ANIMALS

Giant toad, crapaud, kwappo
Bufo marinus

The crapaud was introduced from Central and South America to eat insect pests in the sugar plantations. This large toad is a dusky brown with blotches of chocolate and beige. It has an amazing digestive system, able to process all manner of toxic, noxious, biting and stinging insects. Ants and beetles are staples. The crapaud himself is a hopping barrel of poison, scrupulously avoided by most predators. But crapauds can even digest other crapauds and will have a go at smaller individuals careless enough to get in the way. Crapauds secrete a viscid white poison from above and behind the eyes. This is so poisonous that over-inquisitive dogs have been killed by it. Indeed, this animal is no friend to the dog, for it has also learned to eat dog food from the back porch. The crapaud is quite at home around people, happy to sit below electric lights at night to gobble the insects that are drawn by the glow.

With all this food, these toads grow to nine inches long and weigh in at over two pounds. Males grow very slowly after they have become sexually mature, but the females keep growing apace and, consequently, they tend to be larger.

Crapauds are generally not up and about during the day. They are quite vulnerable to drying out and find a shady place to hide. But you can often see them at night, especially after rain, soaking up stored heat from paved roads and doing their best to get run over by cars.

© Katie Shears

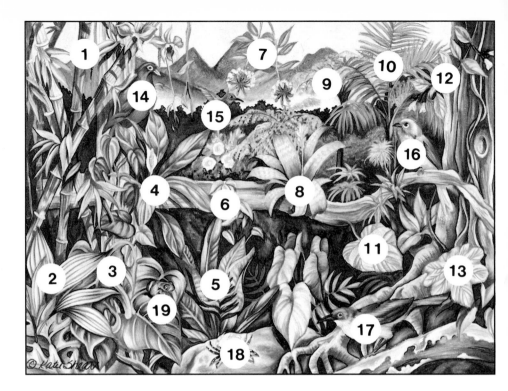

Plants
1. Bamboo
2. Zel mouche
3. Monstera
4. Flowering aroid
5. Heliconia
6. Philodendron
7. Marcgravia umbellata
8. Bromeliad
9. Tree fern
10. Mountain cabbage
11. Fallen balsa leaf
12. Alloplectus cristatus
13. Fallen cecropia leaf

Birds
14. Red-necked pigeon
15. Purple-throated Carib
16. Mountain whistler
17. Trembler

Animals
18. River crab
19. Piping frog

Rainforests are the most luxuriant forests. They grow at middle elevations, unchecked by wind or drought. In the lowland forest, plants struggle against seasonal dryness to survive. High mountain plant communities, called montane and elfin forests, spend much of their time in cloud or rain. It is colder at these upper elevations and the vegetation is stunted by strong buffeting winds. But in the rainforest life is easy and plants of all sizes and shapes have evolved to fill nearly every space and capture almost all the available sunlight. Your eyes become accustomed to the dim light beneath the tall trees, but your camera tells the truth. Undisturbed rainforests can be dark.

Epiphytes -- plants that use other plants for support -- occupy the tree limbs. These botanical squatters exist in temperate forests as well, but only from the moss and lichen groups. In the rainforest epiphytes are from many flowering plant families, including a large number from the beautiful orchid family. Some are enormous, considering that their roots are not in the soil, that they have to store rainwater and that they scavenge nutrients from airborne detritus. Vines and lianas climb up trees. Some plants, like clusia and the strangler fig, climb down trees, for their sticky seeds germinate high in the canopy and their ropy roots dangle, collecting moisture from the air as they entwine themselves in a deadly grip around their host trees.

In the absence of physical restraints to growth, biological controls are highly developed. In the struggle of plant against plant to find a place in the sun, solutions are found which it is hard not to call ingenious. In this ancient, wet and warm environment, the bumbling mechanisms of evolution have produced a large number of highly specialized plants and animals.

Grazing animals are not common in the rainforest and defensive thorns are not needed. Instead, rainforest trees have to deal with predatory insects and their leaves are laced with both bitter and toxic chemicals. It would seem that these are effective since chewed-up leaves are uncommon. Many trees have large buttresses or prop roots which help keep them upright in the soft unstable soils.

J. S. Beard, a forester who inventoried the trees of this region in the 1940's, found 68 tree species that exist only in the Eastern Caribbean, most at higher elevations. Of these, many exist only on one island. The lower dry habitats were connected from Puerto Rico to Antigua during the ice age and many mainland species hopped to the dry areas of Guadeloupe and on down the chain, unifying the lowland flora.

Only a fraction of the original rainforest survives in the Eastern Caribbean. Much of the forest that you will see and which is described in this chapter has been altered by timber harvesting or patch cutting for agriculture. Pioneer species are more common today than they were in the pristine forest. Outside of National Parks, rainforest trees are still being cut to make room for bananas, and often this takes place on very steep hillsides.

Rainforest soils typically have few nutrients. It is hard to believe that this extravagant display of greenery can arise from an impoverished, acid soil, but if you push away the small amount of litter, you will notice that there is virtually no humus, the organic-laden topsoil that is so vital to plant growth in colder climes. Organic matter and nutrients are so quickly and continually harvested by plant roots that the biochemical storeroom is not in the soil, but in the plants themselves. When rainforest is cut down, it is like cutting a temperate forest and scraping up the topsoil at the same time. The heat of the sun on exposed soil exacerbates the problem. Whenever the soil temperature is greater than 77° F (25° C), humus decomposes faster than it is formed and nitrogen goes into the air and is lost.

Like all forests, the rainforest acts as a giant sponge for rainwater, filtering it and releasing it slowly to clear, shaded, cool streams. When too many forest trees are removed, water quality suffers. Crayfish once were a plentiful resource on several islands, but they cannot live in silty water, and some crayfish populations have declined.

Floral displays in the rainforest may disappoint you. The beautiful winter-flowering immortelle seems to many people to be the epitome of the rainforest. It is, however, an introduced tree of sec-ondary forest. Orchids, too, can be spectacularly beautiful, but often are so high in the trees that they appear as mere dots of color. The vivid red bracts of the balisier are a rewarding exception and the colorful hummingbirds which visit them add to the brightness. Look, too, at the varied role of a tree in the rainforest: in addition to the hoards of epiphytes that use it for staging, you may see lizards, small frogs and birds making themselves at home.

Heliconia

PLANTS OF THE AROID FAMILY

Every level of the rainforest has plants from the aroid family. Aroids are in their element, as they do well in dim light and appreciate the continual moisture. Some aroids, such as the Jack-in-the-pulpit and anthurium are best known for their flowers; others, like monstera, don't flower very often. Though all aroid flowers have a similar structure with a spathe and a spadix, the plants are otherwise incredibly varied and grow like the diminutive skunk cabbage poking out of the snow or as the rampant monstera. Some, including many anthuriums, grow normally from the ground and have roots in the soil. Others, like philodendrons, are vines which begin as seeds in the ground, but use trees or other vines for support.

Many plants will climb trees. Spiraling around the trunks and lolling on the branches, they make themselves as completely at home as your least favorite cousin does when he visits your seaside cottage. These vines have leaves (like your cousin, they buy their own food) but they can quickly climb to a place in the sun because they don't need to invest in a support system (they don't pay the mort-

Typical rainforest pool. Note the silvery cecropia leaf lying upside down.

gage) and this makes their lives much easier. To make matters worse for the tree, it may have to invest more in its structure to hold the pesky vine up or it risks having its large branches break.

Swiss cheese plant
Monstera deliciosa

The Swiss cheese plant graces homes and offices everywhere and is probably the best known member of the aroid family. The huge leaves with bizarre perforations are highly unusual and this feature is only rarely found outside of the aroid family. There are 24 monstera species and many of them have holey leaves. The most recent speculation about why a plant would have these holes is that they cause turbulence and keep the leaf cool.

Monstera is a climber and starts life as a seed in the ground. Its tendrils are programmed to reach towards shade as this is the best way to find a tree, its ladder to success. Like many climbers, both in and out of the aroid family, a young monstera's leaves in the dark forest are completely unlike the familiar holey ones. They are small and round and press themselves against the tree trunk. Only when this nondescript vine reaches adequate light levels, does it reveal its extravagant nature and grow its huge, elaborate, lobed leaves.

Most aroid fruits are not edible, but when ripe, the juicy fruiting spadix of *Monstera deliciosa* smells and tastes like banana and pineapple combined and is called ceriman in the West Indies. It can be eaten from the vine or used in desserts.

Wild tobacco, bird's nest anthurium
Anthurium hookeri

This sometimes abundant aroid is an epiphyte, perching on branches, or tucked into the crotch of a tree. The leaves form a loose rosette which funnels water and debris to the dense mat of roots that the plants sits on. Some of the roots grow upwards and penetrate the decaying litter which collects at the leaf bases, extracting nutrients from this built-in compost pile. Wild tobacco flowers have a deep purple spadix and a long, thin green spathe.

Philodendron
Philodendron scandens

Your houseplant is at large in the rainforest - and making the most of its freedom. Philodendron means tree-loving, and these winding climbers take advantage of their lovers. They use a tree as a trellis and zoom right up towards the canopy. If a philodendron grows into an obstacle, it is able to put out a long leafless shoot to act as a feeler, exploring the space around itself with a minimal investment in leaf area. This philodendron rarely flowers. However, broken sections of the stem will root and grow. When philodendron stems dry they are hard and are used as basket handles.

OTHER PLANTS

Bromeliads

Plants of the new world tropics, bromeliads are among the most common epiphytes and some have large flower stalks and beautiful flowers. They are not just found in the rainforest and, in fact, many of the 2000 species are adapted instead to dryness. You can recognize most of them because they look very much like the leafy top of their fellow family member the pineapple, and many bromeliads are called wild pineapple. Spanish moss *(Tillandsia usneoides)*, too, is a bromeliad, though it looks entirely different from most of the rest of its family. It often grows on telephone wires, proving that epiphytes do not depend on a host plant for nutrients. It is unclear whether or not these epiphytes harm trees. They often are abundant on dying trees. Did they shade the tree too much? Or did the tree begin to decline, giving the epiphytes more light in which to flourish?

Having no roots in the soil, an epiphyte is like a house away from city plumbing that collects rainwater from the roof. It also has to find all its own nutrients. Bromeliad leaves are shaped to collect and hold water -- up to 2 gallons of it. From an epiphyte point of view, the rainwater gets even better after insects and micro-organisms move into the storage tank and fallen debris begins to decay in the water providing the plant with a nutritious decaying soup.

Bamboo
Bambusa vulgaris

Bamboo grows in clumps and polished stems spread its feathery foliage outward at the top, like a 40-foot high airy vase of ferns. Trees in size, but grasses in structure, bamboos are not likely to be mistaken for anything else. They were introduced more than a century ago and are sometimes mistakenly called native bamboo. Widely planted to control erosion on roadcuts and streambanks, they do not spread readily on their own because they don't usually grow from seeds. However, they are among the most useful plants in the world and people have seen to their propagation.

There are many bamboo species, most of them difficult to distinguish until they flower. After they flower, which some species do in unison, they die, so you can tell what species a bamboo was, but not what it is.

When all the members of a plant species flower at the same time and produce an enormous crop of seeds at widespread intervals, it is presumed to be a strategy to swamp seed predators. Animals cannot become specialized to eat bamboo seeds, because they are not available often enough. Bamboos carry this strategy to an extreme, with a seeding cycle of up to 120 years. The strategy may have begun back when bamboo precursors flowered irregularly, but not every year. The nutritious seeds only survived being eaten in years when they were abundant. Bamboos that bore fruits in the off years didn't survive. Nowadays, the flowering interval is genetically controlled and clones which are spread around the world from one plant will all flower at the same time.

The strong, hollow, light bamboo stems are widely used in construction. They are also used in some islands to make cassava strainers and fish pots for crayfish. The frames of these beautiful pots are made from the passion flower vine, the string to tie the bamboo on to the frame is made from mahoe.

Cecropia
Cecropia schreberiana

Cecropias are highly visible. Across a valley the silvery undersides of the large leaves stand out against the green background as they are blown by the wind. And underfoot you can often see the deeply-lobed shed leaves, still whitish below. We like to turn them over in search of sheltering frogs and insects.

If you look upwards at a cecropia's leaves you may see that they are riddled with holes. This is one of the few trees on which insect damage is frequently noticeable. These trees don't pack their leaves with the level of defense compounds that other trees go in for. They opt, instead, to grow fast for their survival. Most defense compounds contain nitrogen, a sometimes scarce element which is needed for growth. The holey leaves are soon shed, for the cecropia keeps just a single upper layer in the sun. And how they grow -- eight feet in a year is not unusual, and there is a record of a cecropia that added 16 feet to its height in a single year. The long leafless stem is hollow, which saves on raw materials. The trees often develop stilt roots, useful when soils are unstable. You find them most often on the edges of the rain forest or in clearings, as they need plenty of light.

Another cecropia strategy for success is seed production. Male and female flowers are borne on different trees and a female tree can produce 900,000 seeds each time it fruits. These are lightweight and remain viable in the soil for up to two years. Increased light levels, indicating a gap in the canopy, will trigger germination.

Mountain cabbage. The small red and yellow flowers are wild fuchsia and the palm-like leaves on the bottom right are zel mouche. A cecropia leaf is at the top.

Above: Tree ferns; notice that a bromeliad has managed to get a toe hold on one. Below left: Typical aerial roots of a fig. Below right: wild tobacco.

Sometimes cecropias will be full of a noisy mixed flock of birds, chatting as they gorge themselves on the fruits.

Other names: trumpet tree, bois trompetter, bois canot, bois canon, parasol tree.

Balsa, bois flo
Ochroma pyramidale

Balsa is another fast-growing pioneer. It produces the lightest of all commercial woods, weighing just seven pounds per cubic foot. (The heaviest commercial wood, from lignum vitae, weighs 88.5 pounds per cubic foot.) Balsa means "raft" in Spanish and the wood is used for life rafts, as well as life preservers, floats, toys, for airplane construction, and as insulation. It is easily made into dugout canoes or floating rafts.

When grown for balsa wood, the trees are often harvested at the tender age of about six years old. After this, a heavier wet heartwood develops which is not as desirable as the light colored and light weight sapwood. If left alone, a balsa will become a large tree.

You may see a balsa's big whitish fleshy flowers, either on the tree or on the ground. By the time they reach the ground, they may have turned yellow or brown with age. The big furry fruit capsule looks like a rabbit's foot and contains many small light seeds. The seeds have long hairs attached to them and are carried far by the wind.

Marcgravia, liane a chasseur
Marcgravia umbellata

Marcgravia is a vine with an extraordinary collection of flowers. Like an odd botanical chandelier, marcgravia has about 25 flowers in a circle. In the middle of the circle, ten little bud vases hang in a ring and each is full of liquid. The elegant structure is designed to dust hummingbird backs with pollen when they come for a drink.

This is another plant which has two leaf types. In its tree-climbing youth, it has small leaves, appressed to the tree trunk. Later the leaves are large and free. As with many climbing vines, the first-formed leaves drop off after the plant is established. The leafless stems of similar vines often make a tortuous tangle in the understory which could be described as creepy.

Wild fuchsia
Alloplectus cristatus

On a rainforest walk you may well see the brilliantly colored flowers of this tree-climbing vine. It is native to the West Indies and frequently encountered in moist situations. Both the flower and the calyx (the base of the flower) are showy, but the striking red calyx is far longer-lived than the bright yellow flower, which soon drops to the ground. The thick downy leaves have silvery undersides.

Other names: crete a coq, fuchsia sauvage.

Strangler fig
Ficus citrifolia

Most rainforest plants have a long, tedious struggle to grow from the forest floor into the lighted canopy, but the strangler fig doesn't play by the rules. Its seed sprouts right up at the top of a host tree in bright light, then it slowly kills and takes over its host. In Spanish a strangler fig is a matapalo, which means "tree killer."

Strangler fig fruits are relished by birds and the excreted seeds are very sticky. They adhere to branches high in the canopy, where there is plenty of light. This is not the only clever adaptation these seeds have. Another is that the seeds will not germinate until the seed coat has been corroded by bacterial action which only happens when enough debris has collected to ensure that the seedling will be surrounded by at least a minimum of nutrients. From germination on, this fig's roots grow and grow, first around the branch that the seed has landed on, and then downward around the trunk, or dropping through the air. These downward-growing roots are often mistaken for the stems of vines and lianas growing upwards. They branch and weave themselves around the host tree, growing ever fatter until they grow into each other. Eventually the host tree is strangled and begins to rot away. By this time the fig's roots have welded to each other, forming a hefty woven tube, and have penetrated the earth, so that they completely replace the host tree. It may take 100 years for a fig to kill its host and become fully independent.

Figs can be found in several habitats and they depend on tiny wasps to pollinate their flowers. Female wasps lay eggs in fig flower receptacles. The larvae develop and emerge from a tiny hole in the receptacle that holds the flowers, coating themselves with pollen as they leave. These emerging females seek out other fig flower receptacles in which to lay their eggs and they pollinate the flowers at the same time. The amazing thing about this system is that each of the 800 or so species of fig has its very own wasp species.

It is said that the thick growth of fine hanging roots on the figs of Barbados inspired Portuguese explorers to call them 'las barbados,' the bearded ones. The name then got transferred to the island. Not all figs are killers and not only figs kill by strangling. Clusias, though very different in appearance, strangle trees by the same method.

Other names: bearded fig, figuier.

Clusia
Clusia rosea

Clusia follows the same pattern as the strangler fig. The seed germinates high in the canopy and the roots encircle the host tree. When the roots reach the ground, they use this new energy source to grow yet more avidly, tightening

their grip on the host, until it slowly expires. Other roots dangle freely from clusia and sometimes climbing vines take advantage of them.

Clusia has beautiful creamy to pink flowers and leathery leaves which are dark green above and a dull yellow green on the undersides. The leaves make reasonably good writing paper, which perhaps inspired the name Scotch attorney. Or the name may have been applied by someone with a jaundiced view of the lawyer-client relationship who imagined it to resemble the interaction between clusia and the host tree. The seeds are enclosed in reddish capsules, two or three inches long. They are an important food source for parrots.

It is said that if you smoke your house by burning nine clusia leaves, nine pieces of charcoal and a pack of sulfur, evil spirits will stay away for three months. The sticky sap has been used both medicinally and for caulking boats.

Other names: aralie, awalie, autograph tree, gros pomme, kaklen, Scotch attorney.

Gommier
Dacryodes excelsa

Gommiers must have good deep root systems, for they often grow on steep slopes, and when blasted by hurricanes, the tops usually break before the tree is uprooted. The somewhat bedraggled tree leafs out again. A gommier which has not been knocked back by hurricanes will often have 60 feet of trunk without branches, which increases its value as a timber tree.

Gommiers do not have the big buttresses that characterize chataigners - the other important timber tree of the islands. But they do usually have a bulge at the base. If the thick gray bark is injured, an aromatic gum oozes out. The gum is used for incense in churches, for torches and to ignite charcoal fires.

The leaves are usually too high to see,

but they have five to seven leaflets. The fruits are eaten by parrots. The gommier is a true West Indian tree, native from Puerto Rico to Grenada, adapted to the slopes and the weather, and much used by local people for centuries.

The gommier was the tree of choice for Carib canoes and the tradition, slightly altered, continues today. A giant tree is hollowed out with an axe. The Caribs used stone axes and this part of the process took them several weeks. After this, and while the tree is still green, branches are inserted to widen the boat, and it is filled with water to keep it limber while it is stretched out. Planks are added to the sides of the carved-out gommier log to increase the freeboard of the canoe by six to eight inches. Modern canoes are equipped with powerful outboard motors and are often seen fishing far out at sea. Canoe comes from the word "canoa," which means a boat made from a single timber. Some say that it was the first word from the Americas to be used in Europe.

Other names: gommier blanc, mountain gommier, bois gommier, gommier a canots.

Heliconia, balisier
Heliconia caribaea

Most heliconias do right by their name, which means "sun-loving." They grow vigorously, to 12 feet high, in gaps in the rainforest. Heliconias love moisture as well as sun and will often be at their best on a sunny streambank. Related to bananas, they have big paddle-shaped leaves whose rolled bases form a low stem. The flower stalk rises banana-like from the center and the vivid yellow or red bracts look as though they were carved from wood and then painted. Hummingbirds fight with each other to get at the nectar from the tiny flowers that bloom within the bracts. Other birds eat the blue berries and distribute the seeds.

Heliconia leaves are used to cover bread as it rises, for thatching and to line baskets.

Zel mouche
Cardoluvica insignis

This species grows on the ground, but a common close relative clambers up trees. They are very common plants and look like young palm trees: the leaves have bold parallel veins and are divided into two lobes. No rainforest would be complete without its zel mouche. Baskets are made from the roots and the leaves are used to line the baskets. The leaves are also used for thatching temporary shelters.

Other names: z' ailes mouches, ti kanot.

Tree fern
Cyathea arborea

Tree ferns make a magnificent first impression and early visitors to the tropics were overwhelmed when they first saw these large trees. They are often over 20 feet high, and all the delicate laciness and charm of the small ferns is carried to this grand scale. The straight single stem rises leafless from the forest floor and is topped by the large airy fronds. They are easily recognized as ferns, for the fronds uncoil from fiddleheads, a habit peculiar to ferns.

Tree ferns look like ordinary ferns at first. They grow to their full diameter at ground level before they begin to rise. Once they start their upward journey, they lose a leaf for every new one that unrolls from the apex. Epiphytes are shed with the old leaves and tree ferns almost always look fresh and perfect. In the Caribbean they grow abundantly in disturbed areas such as road cuts, landslides or in gaps in the forest, whether created from tree cutting or cleared to grow crops. There are several species. The closely related *Cyathea imrayana* has spines on the trunk and leaf stems. Millions of years ago tree ferns like these were a major part of the earth's vegetation.

Not everyone appreciates tree ferns. The leaves are almost never eaten by insects and cattle turn up their noses if fronds are offered as fodder.

Mountain cabbage
Prestoea montana

Mountain cabbage is the most common palm in the rainforest and is even more prevalent at higher elevations. A startlingly pink, big brushy flower cluster sprouts from below the leaves. Half inch dark red fruits form at the ends of the cluster's branches. This is a slow growing tree which produces only one to four of its giant leaves each year. The slender trunk is

upright and straight and the tree eventually will grow to 30 feet.

The main bud is sometimes used in salads, but its removal kills the tree.

Other names: palmiste chou, mountain palm.

BIRDS

Purple throated carib, colibri rouge
Eulampis jugularis

This is a dark hummingbird, but in the proper light its purple-red throat glows like a lantern. The wings and tail are a metallic green. Purple-throated caribs are most often seen in the forest, but will venture into banana plantations. Like most hummingbirds, they are not particularly afraid of humans and will sometimes allow a close approach. Perhaps their exceptional flying abilities give them confidence.

Pearly-eyed thrasher
Margarops fuscatus

The pearly-eyed thrasher is an aggressive bird, considered by some to be a threat to the islands' parrot species. These thrashers use the same kinds of nesting holes as parrots and have been known to eat parrot eggs. If tree cavities are not available, they will build a bulky nest. They have been described by ornithologists as "tramps," a somewhat derogatory characterization, based on their ability to thrive in many different situations. Though most often seen in the rainforest, pearly-eyed thrashers will also use tree plantations and secondary forests.

One thing that contributes to a species being labelled a tramp is its ability to eat almost anything. These thrashers eat a wide variety of fruits or insects, depending on what is available. They will feed in the canopy and are fond of cecropia fruits, but are more often seen scratching among leaves on the forest floor. They have a high reproductive potential, raising multiple broods each year.

Pearly-eyed thrashers are a mix of brown and gray-brown and have long tails. The breast is lighter, changing from darkish brown under the throat to white on the belly, with scale-like brown markings.

Other names: grosse grive, paw-paw bird.

Red-necked pigeon
Columba squamosa

The red-necked pigeon, too, uses a variety of habitats, but is most often seen in the rainforest. It is the biggest dove in the islands, growing to 15 inches long, and is stout-bodied, with a short neck and small head -- like other pigeons. The short slender bill thickens towards the tip. A red-necked pigeon is basically dark gray with a dull purple head and some metallic purple on the nape of the neck.

Most pigeons are sleek, powerful flyers with a thick, heavy coat of strong-shafted feathers that are so loosely attached to their thin skins that they drop out very easily, perhaps as a protective mechanism against certain predators. Their soft plaintive cooing can become monotonously repetitive. Their food is almost entirely vegetable matter: seeds, grains, and fruits are favorites.

They build a flimsy platform of sticks in a tree. Both parents incubate the eggs; the female by day, and the male at night. Both feed the young on what is known as pigeon's milk. During the incubation period the lining of the pigeon's crop thickens, and when the young are ready to be fed, the lining sloughs off into a cheesy curd which the parents regurgitate into the young. It has much the same food value as mammals' milk. Later, partially digested seeds are added to the chicks' diet.

Other names: rammier, scaly-naped pigeon, mountain pigeon, wanmye.

Mountain whistler
Myadestes genibarbis

The mountain whistler is well known for its song, a thin plaintive whistle which carries across wide valleys. These birds live on the highest mountains but also occur in the more moderate terrain of the rainforest. Though much more often heard than seen, a lucky few will see a small thrush-like bird, mostly a slaty gray, but with a striking reddish throat. Mountain whistlers feed on berries and insects.

Other names: rufous-throated solitaire, sifle moutayn.

Trembler
Cinclocerthia ruficauda

Tremblers only live in the Lesser Antilles, mostly at rainforest elevations. Their eyes are a striking orange-yellow color. They have long slender down-turned bills and dark brown to olive gray upper parts. The underparts are paler, varying from grayish-brown to grayish white. There are differences in trembler coloring from island to island, and if these birds are ever studied carefully, it may be found that there is more than one species. The trembler has two peculiar habits: it holds its tail straight up and it shivers and trembles.

Tremblers are quiet birds, but when they are in the mood they sing a series of notes, some melodious and others harsh. They nest in tree cavities, in tree ferns, or at base of palm fronds. Sometimes they will nest in a bromeliad. They usually nest between March and August. These shy birds have declined because of forest destruction.

ANIMALS

Piping frog
Eleuthero-dactylus johnstonei

This particular frog lives on 15 islands in the Lesser Antilles and there are other species of little pipers on other islands. This frog is tan, usually less than an inch long and is heard far more often than it is seen. The sweet two-note call mixes with evening insect sounds to enrich the tropical night.

Small clutches of eggs are laid on the moist forest floor, under a stone or a fallen tree, and they are guarded by the female. The embryos pass through a highly modified tadpole stage while still in the egg and, two weeks later, hatch as tiny froglets. The quarter inch long little ones cut their way out of the egg with a special egg tooth at the tips of their noses. These frogs sing all day in the rainforest, where it is damp; in drier areas they sing only at night. It is only the male that calls. If you are patient, you may be able to track a singing frog down and see the skin of its little throat puff out with every note.

River crab
Guinotia dentata

The yellow and brown river crab is often found in or near rainforest streams and rivers, and it can remain underwater for a long period of time. These crabs are

140

much sought after for food. The crab meat is added to calaloo soup.

Just as piping frog offspring skip the swimming tadpole stage, so the river crabs skip the many larval stages which most crabs pass through at sea. This is one of the few land crabs that is truly independent of the sea. A female river crab carries her fertilized eggs on her abdomen where a hard abdominal flap gives them some protection. All the larval stages take place within the embryo and when the little crabs hatch, they look very much like miniature models of their parents. The babies cling to their mother for a while, before striking out on their own. River crabs excavate beneath stones or dig burrows and retreat to avoid predators.

Other names: siwik, cirique.

MISCELLANEOUS NOTES

A NOTE TO VISITORS

The best thing the Caribbean visitor can do to help the environment is to enjoy it. Local economies respond to tourist dollars, and when those dollars are spent visiting rainforests and mangroves, the value of these unspoiled natural areas is recognized.

Buying local handicrafts is very help-ful to island economies. Buy products from easily renewable resources such as wood, coconut shells and husks, calabash and seeds. Buying locally made baskets, batiks and paintings also helps islanders. Avoid buying anything made from coral or turtle shell.

HIKING IN THE ISLANDS

Many islands have conservation organizations or National Trusts and the staff of these organizations may have ideas about interesting areas for you to visit. In many islands the forestry departments have built nature trails and printed trail maps. "The Outdoor Traveler's Guide: Caribbean," by Kay Showker, published by Stewart, Tabori and Chang, NY, (1989) is a beauti-fully-produced guide which covers all of the Caribbean.

WHAT'S IN A LATIN NAME?

In this book we have given both common and Latin names. Since there are often many common names for a single species, and many common names are used for more than one species, common names can be hopelessly confusing. Latin names are much clearer, with only one name applying to one species world-wide, but the disadvantage is that few people know them.

For those unfamiliar with Latin names, here are some basics: Two names are needed to define a species: a genus name which generally refers to a group of species and a specific epithet, often called the species name, which refers an individual species. Thus *Aloe barbadensis* is a species, *Aloe* is the genus name and *barbadensis* is the specific epithet. Latin names are generally italicized or printed in bold type. The genus always begins with a capital letter and the specific epithet usually does not. Plant families are usually larger groupings of several genera.

Latin names are given by the first person to publish a report on a newly discovered genus or species and deposit a specimen of the plant in a herbarium. That person can choose the name, but it is always "Latinized." Sometimes the name refers to the person who discovered the plant. Thus *Bougainvillea* came from Louis de Bougainville. At other times the name refers to the plant's home (*madagascariensis*), the habitat where the plant comes from (*montana*), or some property of the plant (*pulcherrima* means very handsome).

While there are never two current Latin names for a plant, Latin names can change.

This happens when an earlier valid name is discovered. This can occur even after a name has been in use for many years. Thus the long-used *Aloe vera* has become *Aloe barbadensis*, much to the dismay of some horticulturists.

The Latin names of plants are often followed by a reference to the person who first categorized the plant and to the person who reclassified it at a later time. Since this book is intended to be an introductory guide and not a taxonomic reference, we have ignored this convention.

REFERENCES

Amato, Ivan. 1990. Smart as a Brick. Science News, March 10.

Anonymous. No date given. Union Nature Trail Medicinal Garden. Forestry Department, St. Lucia.

Beard, J. S. 1949. The Natural Vegetation of the Windward and Leeward Islands. Oxford Forestry Memoirs, No.21. The Clarendon Press, Oxford, UK.

Bond, James. 1971. Birds of the West Indies. Collins Press, London, UK.

Brower, Kenneth. 1988. State of the Reef. Audubon, March.

Brown, Deni. 1988. Aroids: Plants of the Arum Family. Timber Press, Portland, OR.

Brucher, Heinz. 1989. Useful Plants of Neotropical Origin and their Wild Relatives. Springer-Verlag, Berlin.

Burns, Russell M. and Barbara H. Honkala. 1990. Silvics of North America. USDA Forest Service, Washington, DC.

Corner, E. J. H. 1966. The Natural History of Palms, University of California Press, CA.

Correll, Donovan S. 1982. Flora of the Bahamas. J. Cramer, Vaduz.

Evans, Peter G. H. 1990. Birds of the Eastern Caribbean. Macmillan Education Ltd., London, UK.

Everett, Thomas H. 1981. The New York Botanical Garden Illustrated Encyclopedia of Horticulture. Garland Publishing, NY.

Faaborg, J. R. and W. J. Arendt. 1985. Wildlife Assessments in the Caribbean, Institute of Tropical Forestry, Rio Peidras, PR.

Forsyth, Adrian and Ken Miyata. 1984. Tropical Nature. Charles Scribner's Sons, NY.

Fournet, Jacques. 1977. Plants and Flowers of the Caribbean. Les Editions du Pacifique, Papeete, Tahiti.

Gans, Carl, and F. H. Pough, eds. 1982. Biology of the Reptilia. Academic Press, London, UK.

Grech, Maria. 1989. Bush Talk, a series of publications for the Forestry Management and Conservation Project, Ministry of Agriculture, St. Lucia.

Groome, John R. 1970. A Natural History of the Island of Grenada, W.I. Caribbean Printers Ltd. Arima, Trinidad.

Henry, E.T. 1990. Hawsbill Sea Turtle, Eag'er, Environmental awareness group, Antgua, October.

Holm-Nielsen, L. B., et al., eds. 1989. Tropical Forests. Academic Press, Harcourt Brace, NY.

Honychurch, Penelope N. 1980. Caribbean Wild Plants and their Uses. Macmillan Publishers Ltd., London, UK.

Howard, Richard A. 1974-1989. Flora of the Lesser Antilles. Arnold Arboretum, Jamaica Plain, MA.

Huey, Raymond B., Eric R. Pianka, and Thomas W. Schoener. 1983. Lizard Ecology: Studies of a model organism. Harvard University Press, Cambridge, MA.

Humann, Paul. 1989. Reef Fish Identification. New World Publications, Jacksonville, FL.

Humann, Paul. 1992. Reef Creature Identification. New World Publications, Jacksonville, FL.

Janzen, Daniel H., ed. 1993. Costa Rica Natural History. University of Chicago Press, Chicago, IL.

Johnson, Timothy H. 1991. Biodiversity and Conservation in the Caribbean: Profiles of Selected Islands, International Council for Bird Preservation, Monograph No. 1, Cambridge, UK.

Kaplan, Eugene H. 1982. A Field Guide to Southeastern and Caribbean Seashores. Peterson Field Guide Series, Houghton Mifflin Company, Boston, MA.

Kaplan, Eugene H. 1988. A Field Guide to Coral Reefs: Caribbean and Florida. Peterson Field Guide Series, Houghton Mifflin Company, Boston, MA.

Kimber, Clarissa T. 1988. Martinique Revisited: The Changing Plant Geographies of a West Indian Island. Texas A & M University Press, College Station, TX.

Kingsbury, John M. 1988. 200 Conspicuous, Unusual, or Economically Important Tropical Plants of the Caribbean. Bullbrier Press, Ithaca, NY.

Kricher, John C. 1989. A Neotropical Companion. Princeton University Press, Princeton, NJ.

Little, Elbert L., Jr., and Frank H. Wadsworth. 1974. Trees of Puerto Rico and the Virgin Islands. USDA Forest Service, Washington, DC.

Little, Elbert L., Jr., and Frank H. Wadsworth. 1989. Common Trees of Puerto Rico and the Virgin Islands. Reprinted privately by the authors, Washington, DC.

Long, Earl G. 1974. The Serpent's Tale: Reptiles and Amphibians of St. Lucia, University of the West Indies, St. Lucia.

Long, Robert W. and Olga Lakela. 1971. A Flora of Tropical Florida, University of Florida Press, Gainesville, FL.

Murphy, Peter G. 1986. Structure and biomass of a subtropical dry forest in Puerto Rico, Biotropica 18(2): 89-96.

Myers, Ronald L., and John J. Ewel, eds. 1990. Ecosystems of Florida. University of Central Florida Press, Orlando, FL.

National Research Council (U.S.) Committee on Sea Turtle Conservation. 1990. Decline of the Sea Turtles: Causes and Prevention. National Academy Press, Washington, DC.

Nobel, Park S. 1988. Environmental Biology of Agaves and Cacti. Cambridge University Press, Cambridge, UK.

Ogden, John C. 1980. "Faunal relationships in Caribbean seagrass beds," in Handbook of Seagrass Biology: an Ecosystem Perspective, edited by R. C. Phillips and C. P. McRoy, Garland STPM Press, NY.

Purseglove, J. W. 1968. Tropical Crops: Dicotoledons, John Wiley & Sons, NY.

Purseglove, J. W. 1972. Tropical Crops: Monocotyledons, John Wiley & Sons, NY.

Reimold, R. J. and W. H. Queen, eds. 1974. Ecology of Halophytes, Academic Press, NY.

Schwartz, Albert and Robert W. Henderson. 1991. Amphibians and Reptiles of the West Indies. University of FL Press, Gainesville, FL.

Stamps, Judy. 1990. Starter homes for young lizards. Natural History, October.

Tomlinson, P. B. 1986. The Botany of Mangroves, Cambridge University Press, Cambridge, UK.

Warner, Robert R. 1988. Boys Will be Boys. Natural History, April.

Warren W. Burggren and Brian R. McMahon, eds. 1988. Biology of the Land Crabs, Cambridge University Press, Cambridge, UK.

Wilson, R. and J. Q. Wilson. 1985. Watching Fishes, Harper and Row, NY.

Wolcott, Thomas G. and Donna L. Wolcott. 1990. Wet Behind the Gills. Natural History, October.

INDEX

Bold numbers indicate photographs

148